Ninja Dual
Air Fryer
Recipe Book UK

Ninja Dual Air Fryer Recipes and 30-Day Meal Plan to Help You
Cook More Delicious Food from All Over the World

Georgia Chambers

Table of Contents

Introduction

The Ninja Foodi 2-Basket Air Fryer is a revolutionary cooking system with two baskets for maximum versatility. Thanks to its 8-quart capacity and Dual Zone technology, it enables you to cook two items in two different ways simultaneously. Each of the two 4-quart cooking zones has its cooking basket, cyclonic fan, and rapid heater to provide you with maximum cooking flexibility. With six cooking functions - max crisp, air fry, bake, roast, dehydrate, and reheat - you can mix and match to get the perfect meal. Plus, the two baskets are non-stick, and the crisper plates are dishwasher-safe, so they're easy to clean. Unleash the power of the Ninja Foodi 2-Basket Air Fryer and enjoy maximum cooking convenience.

The Ninja Foodi 2-Basket Air Fryer is ideal for busy adults who need to prepare a meal quickly. With two baskets, you can prepare two dishes at once – like air-frying potatoes in one basket and roasting a chicken in another. This unique feature has been a real game-changer for my family. With this powerful appliance, you can make nearly an entire meal in no time – saving you time and effort.

Fundamentals of Ninja Foodi 2-Basket Air Fryer

The revolutionary Ninja Foodi Dual Zone 2-Basket Air Fryer is the first air fryer to feature two separate baskets for cooking two different items simultaneously! With its Smart Finish function and Match Cook button, you can quickly copy settings between both baskets to fully use the 8-qt capacity of this Dual Zone Technology. With six programmable options – Air Fried, Air Broiled, Roasted, Baked, Reheated, and Dehydrated – you can easily prepare large quantities of French fries and chicken wings for a crowd. The extra-large 8-quart capacity also ensures even greater convenience and flexibility. The two separate 4-quart areas have their own set of frying baskets, cyclonic fans, and speedy warmers. At the same time, the wide operating temperature range of 105°F to 450°F allows you to cook with precision and accuracy. With the Ninja Foodi Dual Zone 2-Basket Air Fryer, you can enjoy efficient, professional results every time.

What Is Ninja Foodi 2-Basket Air Fryer?

The Ninja Foodi 2-Basket Air Fryer stands out from the crowd for several reasons. It's one of the first air fryers on the market with two baskets, allowing busy families to cook two dishes and have them both ready simultaneously. Although it has a higher price tag, the Ninja brand of kitchen appliances is known for its high-quality construction, so it's worth the investment. Coffee machines, kitchen appliances, pressure cookers, and air fryers are all produced to the highest standards by Ninja. The Ninja Foodi 2-Basket Air Fryer offers all the health benefits of a traditional deep-fryer, such as achieving the same crunchiness and tenderness but without the need to switch between the oven and the stove. The sleek, matte grey and black color scheme are easy to clean and looks great in any kitchen. Plus, the two separate baskets let you prepare two dishes at once, so you can get dinner on the table quickly and easily.

Feature of Ninja Foodi 2-Basket Air Fryer

1. The Ninja Foodi 2-Basket Air Fryer is an advanced kitchen appliance designed to help you easily create delicious meals.

2. This two-basket air fryer has extensive temperature options, ranging from 105 degrees to 450 degrees, and can be used to oven fry, air grill, broil, roast, reheat, and dehydrate Food.

3. The dual-zone technology of this air fryer enables you to replicate preferences in both areas, with each zone having its temperature and ventilation controlled independently with cyclonic fans and instantaneous heaters.

4. Smart Finish technology allows you to coordinate cooking times in each zone automatically. You can cook two things in two different methods and finish them simultaneously.

5. For perfect, even browning and crisping, the Ninja Foodi 2-Basket Air Fryer also includes two nonstick crisper plates. And for added convenience, these nonstick dinnerware sets are safe to be cleaned in the dishwasher.

6. Experience delicious, professional-level results with the Ninja Foodi 2-Basket Air Fryer. Enjoy the convenience of creating your favorite meals with ease.

Control Keys of Ninja Foodi 2-Basket Air Fryer

Manages the output to the left basket.

Regulates the flow to the right basket.

TEMP Arrows

Before or during Cooking, you can use the up-and-down arrows to adjust the oven's temperature to your desired setting conveniently. With this simple feature, you can ensure your Food is cooked to perfection every time.

TIME Arrows

Using the up and down arrows before the cooking process, you can easily adjust the cooking time of any function to suit your needs. This flexibility allows you to customize your cooking experience, giving you the professional control you desire.

SMART FINISH Button

Syncing cook timings has never been more accessible! Our advanced timer ensures both zones of your kitchen are cooked perfectly and simultaneously, even if they require different times. Our professional timer guarantees that your meal is cooked to perfection.

Match Cook Button

By pressing the MATCH COOK button, you can easily match the function, heat, and time settings in zone 2 to those in zone 1. This will allow you to cook the same item or a variety of other foods simultaneously, making meal prep more convenient. With professional-grade accuracy, you can cook with confidence and enjoy delicious results.

Start/ Pause Button

Press the START/PAUSE button to begin cooking once you've set the desired temperature and time. Ready to take a break? Just click the START/PAUSE button and select the zone you'd like to pause. Professional and efficient, you'll be able to enjoy a break from cooking with ease.

The POWER Button

This Power button activates or deactivates the machine, halting all cooking processes. In standby mode, the device will enter sleep mode after 10 minutes, emitting a dim light. Professional and reliable, this button ensures the safety and efficiency of your cooking process.

Hold Mode

While in SMART Finishing mode, the machine will display the word "Hold." To ensure precise timing, one zone will fry while the other holds. This professional-grade process guarantees the most effective results.

Functions of Ninja Foodi 2-Basket Air Fryer

The Ninja Foodi 2-Basket Air Fryer is a real blessing for large families, thanks to its six fully digitalized functions that make cooking dinner a breeze. With its dual baskets and crisper plates, large families can now enjoy perfectly fried Food with minimal effort. This professional-grade air fryer is perfect for busy adults who want to make the most of their time in the kitchen.

Air Broil

The Air broil function is the perfect way to get the crispiest, healthiest Food with minimal oil. You can perfectly cook frozen foods, patties, chips, and meat without worrying about extra calories. With this advanced technology, you can get delicious meals that are both flavorful and healthy. Professional chefs and home cooks alike will love the convenience and results of this revolutionary cooking method.

Air Fry

The Ninja Foodi 2-basket air fryer is the perfect solution for those who love fried foods but don't want the guilt that comes with it. This appliance uses little to no oil, allowing you to indulge in your favorite fried foods without all the extra calories. You can enjoy all the flavor of fried Food without the added guilt, knowing that it eliminates up to 70% of the calories in fried foods! So go ahead and satisfy your cravings with the peace of mind that you're not consuming unhealthy fats.

Roast

With the dual baskets on this roaster, you can roast your vegetables and meats simultaneously - so you'll get more of your favorite dishes done in less time. And because the baskets don't sacrifice texture, your roasted foods will come out perfectly cooked every time. So, get the most out of your meal prep with this professional-grade roaster.

Reheat

The reheat function on your oven or stovetop is an efficient and convenient way to enjoy your Food just as if it had been freshly cooked. It allows you to warm up meals without compromising their taste or texture, giving you the perfect meal every time. With this function, you can ensure that your meals are as delicious and delicious-looking as the day you prepared them - no matter how long ago that was.

Dehydrate

Dehydration is an effective food preservation method that helps you maintain a healthy lifestyle. You can dry fruits, vegetables, and meat for snacking by using the dehydrate function on your kitchen appliances. This allows you to

store extra Food and prevent it from going to waste. With this great function, you can also create chips from citrus fruits, meat, and vegetables. So, take advantage of this professional-grade dehydrate function and make delicious snacks that last!

Bake

The Ninja Foodi 2-basket air fryer is the perfect conventional oven for baking delicious desserts. With its powerful bake function, you can create all kinds of desserts, tarts, cookies, puddings, and creamy treats. It also lets you maintain a steady temperature so you can bake two sweet and savory desserts in a single turn. Whether you're a professional chef or a home baker, the Ninja Foodi 2-basket air fryer is the perfect tool for baking delicious desserts.

Before First Use

To ensure your safety and the proper functioning of your unit, please follow these instructions carefully:

1. Remove all packing materials, marketing materials, and tapes from the unit.
2. Remove all attachments from the packaging.
3. Pay great attention to operational directions, cautions, and vital precautions to prevent property damage or injury.
4. Wash the baskets plates in hot water and soap, then rinse and dry thoroughly. The sharper dishes and hampers are the only washer elements to be washed. Do not wash the central unit inside the washer.
5. For your safety and to ensure the proper unit functioning, please follow these instructions carefully.

Step-By-Step Ninja Foodi 2-Basket Air Fryer

Dual Zone Technology

Dual Zone Technology is the perfect tool for busy people who want the convenience of different cooking options. Two distinct zones allow you to cook other dishes simultaneously – ideal for big family meals or special occasions. Bright Finish ensures that both are ready to serve simultaneously, no matter the difference in settings. To ensure you're getting the most out of this feature, please refer to pages 10–13 for detailed instructions on how to use each function.

Achieve a perfectly cooked meal with SMART FINISH. With this feature, you can cook multiple dishes at once, even if the cooking times, temperatures, and functions are different for each Food. Perfect for busy adults, SMART FINISH provides professional results in a fraction of the time.

● Put the Food in the baskets, then place them into the unit.
● Light will stay on in Zone 1, where you can choose the cooking function you wish to use. Adjust the temperature
● with the TEMP arrows and set the time with the TIME arrows. For Zone 2, select the cooking function you would

like to use

- Set the temperature with the TEMP arrows and the time with the TIME arrows. Click SMART FINISH, and then press START/PAUSE to start cooking in the zone with the longest time.
- The Hold sign will appear in the other zone. Even if both zones have the same time remaining, the unit will make a noise and turn on the second zone. When the Cooking is complete, the device will beep, and 'End' will display on the screen.
- Remove the ingredients carefully, pouring them out or using tongs or other tools with silicone tips. Do not place the drawer on the unit's top.

Match Cook

Cook more and enjoy a greater variety of dishes with the same functionality, temperature, and time. With the same ease and efficiency, you can now prepare a wider assortment of meals for the whole family to enjoy. Professional Cooking has never been easier.

- Insert the ingredients into the baskets, then insert the baskets into the unit. In Zone 1, the lights will stay on for an additional two minutes.
- Select the desired cooking mode - the AIR BROIL command is unavailable in this zone. You can modify the temperature using the TEMP arrows and adjust the time with the TIME arrows. For Zone 2, utilize the MATCH COOK key to mirror the parameters of Zone 1.
- Once both zones are ready to begin cooking, press the START/PAUSE button. When the cooking period is finished, "End" will flash on both displays simultaneously.
- Finally, use tongs or tools with silicone tips to remove the ingredients from the unit or drop them out.

Both zones start at once but terminate at separate times:

- If you're looking to start cooking quickly, Zone 1 is the perfect place. Adjust the temperature with the TEMP buttons and the time with the TIME arrows. Then, repeat these steps for Zone 2. Keep in mind an AIR BROIL cannot be set in Zone 1. To kick off Cooking in both zones, press the START/PAUSE button.

When the cooking cycle in each zone is finished, the unit will let out a buzz and show "End" on the screen.

Then, ingredients can be removed easily by dropping them out or using tongs or tools with silicone tips.

No matter your cooking needs, this is a professional and easy way to start.

Benefits of Ninja Foodi 2-Basket Air Fryer

Healthy Cooking

The Ninja Foodi 2-Basket Air Fryer is the perfect solution for those who want to cook healthier meals. Its advanced cooking process uses very little oil, making it an ideal way to replace deep-fried foods with something more nutritious. With minimal oil to coat your favorite breaded chicken tenders or fried fish, you can still enjoy a satisfyingly crunchy texture without all the unhealthy fat. And you don't need to fry French fries or tater tots deep to get that crispy golden-brown exterior. Enjoy a healthier meal with the Ninja Foodi 2-Basket Air Fryer.

Easy to Use
The Ninja Foodi 2-Basket Air Fryer was created as an alternative to deep fryers, as most people don't need to use them regularly. Ready-made meals and takeout may be convenient, but home-cooked meals are healthier and more enjoyable. With the Ninja Foodi Air Fryer, you can easily and quickly prepare delicious meals—such as salmon, chicken, and pork roasts—in less than 20 minutes. This professional-grade air fryer makes cooking meals from the comfort of your home more accessible and enjoyable. With the Ninja Foodi Air Fryer, you'll save time and money and enjoy healthier meals.

Crispy oil-free Food
For those who often prepare frozen and breaded meals like onion poppers and chicken tenders, the Ninja Foodi 2-Basket Air Fryer is the ideal way to cook. This air fryer crisps the Food's exterior with just a bit of cooking oil, giving it a crunchy, golden finish instead of a soggy mess. Plus, it's the perfect way to reheat leftover pizzas, making the bottom crust crunchy while bringing the toppings back to life. With the Ninja Foodi 2-Basket Air Fryer, you can enjoy your favorite frozen and breaded meals as excellently as they were on the first day.

Versatile
The Ninja Foodi 2-Basket Air Fryer is the perfect solution for busy people looking for a healthier alternative to deep frying. It is a great way to cook frozen foods like French fries, soft tacos, and pizza rolls, but it can also handle a wide range of meals - from fried chicken to whole butternut squash to sauces and even sweets. And it's so simple that even children can use it to whip up a delicious dinner. With the Ninja Foodi 2-Basket Air Fryer, you'll be able to cook healthier meals easily and quickly.

Fast and perfect Cooking
The Ninja Foodi 2-Basket Air Fryer is an incredibly efficient cooking tool. With its rapid heating capability and high temperatures, you can quickly and evenly cook your meals. Not only do you save time, but the circulating air helps to brown and crisp your Food without you having to do much extra work. Unlike ovens, most recipes don't require any preheating time for an air fryer. This means you can cook faster than ever before—no more waiting 10

minutes for an oven to preheat. With the Ninja Foodi 2-Basket Air Fryer, you can cook confidently, knowing that you'll get the same great results in less time!

Cleaning and Caring for Ninja Foodi 2-Basket Air Fryer

Following each use, it is imperative to give your device a thorough cleaning to ensure its optimal performance. When it comes time to clean your machine, remember always to unplug it from the wall first. This will provide you with a safe and effective cleaning experience.

- **Main Unit:** Using a moist cloth, you can safely and effectively clean the Buy This Product and its control panel. However, it is essential to note that the Buy This Product should never be submerged in any liquid or placed in a dishwasher. Doing so could cause irreparable damage to the device. As a professional, we urge you to take the necessary precautions to ensure your Buy This Product remains in optimal condition.
- **Crisper Plates:** The dishwasher and manual washing are suitable for washing crisper plates. To ensure a thorough clean, we recommend letting the plates dry naturally; however, if you opt to wash them by hand, you can also dry them with a towel. This method is suitable for adults and is the most professional way to ensure your dishes are sparkling clean.
- **Baskets:** For optimal care of your baskets, we recommend hand washing them rather than using a dishwasher. To do so, fill a sink with warm, soapy water and place your plates or baskets from the crisper, allowing the water to loosen any food particles that may be adhered to. Once finished, thoroughly dry all components by letting them air dry or patting them dry with a towel. Hand washing your basket is the best way to ensure its longevity.

Tips for Using Accessories

1. Arrange your components in a single layer on the bottom of the baskets with no overlap to ensure uniform browning. At the midway point, give the ingredients a good shake to ensure nothing is sticking together.
2. For recipe conversions, decrease the heat by 25 degrees Fahrenheit to prevent overcooking. The air fryer's fan can occasionally disperse lighter foodstuffs, so wooden toothpicks can be used to avoid this from happening with things like the sandwich's top bread.

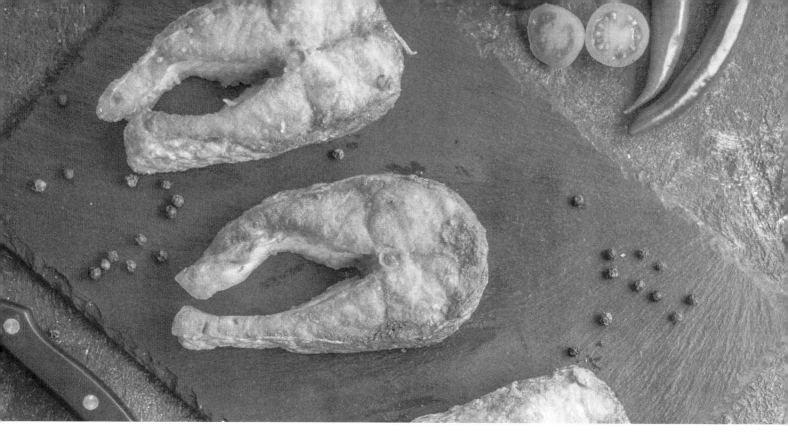

3. The cooking time and temperature can be modified at any point in the cooking process - press the TEMP or TIME buttons, respectively. With a professional tone, use this advice to help you get the best results from your air fryer.

4. Crisper plates lift the contents of the baskets, allowing air to circulate beneath and around the components for uniform crisping. With the START/PAUSE button, you can start cooking immediately after selecting a cooking mode.

5. To ensure optimal performance, be sure to set the time and temperature set points. When cooking fresh veggies and potatoes, creating the perfect crispy dish requires at least one teaspoon of oil.

6. For extra-crispy chips, feel free to add more oil. Be sure to check on the meal frequently throughout the cooking process and remove it once the desired browning has been achieved. T

7. To avoid overcooking proteins, use a thermometer that gives an immediate reading. And remember, when the cooking time is up, remove the Food immediately to prevent it from getting overdone.

Frequently Asked Questions

How I change the time if I only have one zone?

If only one zone is activated, you can easily adjust the time or temperature by using the up and down arrows. This can be done anytime, making your home comfortable and energy efficient. With a professional approach, you can make the necessary changes to ensure your home is always at the desired temperature and time.

How do I change the temperature when both zones are in use?

Choose the temperature or time zone you want, then use the arrows next to TEMP or TIME to adjust the temperature or the time accordingly. With a professional but easy-to-understand tone, you can quickly and easily customize your environment to suit your needs.

Can I cook different things in each zone without getting mixed up?

Yes, all zones are independently operated and feature fans and heating elements, ensuring a comfortable and efficient user experience. Professional care has been taken to ensure that each zone is optimally heated and cooled to meet the needs of adults.

How do I stop one zone once using both zones?

Choose the zone you want to start or stop playing in and press the START/PAUSE button. With this simple button, you can easily control the playtime and take a break whenever needed. Professional and straightforward – it's just that easy.

While air-frying, why do some ingredients fly around?

To ensure optimal performance, it is advised to occasionally use wooden toothpicks to secure food items in your air fryer. This is especially important for lighter foods, such as the top slice of a sandwich, which may be moved around by the air fryer's fan. By using toothpicks, you can be sure that your Food remains securely in place.

Can I air-fry wet and battered things?

A suitable breading method is essential for ensuring that your Food is adequately coated. To ensure the crumbs don't get blown away by the fan, start by coating the item with flour, an egg, and then finally with bread crumbs. Press the breading firmly on the battered items for the best results. Professionalism and attention to detail are crucial to getting the perfect results.

Why didn't the screen show anything?

To resume device operation, press the power button. This will turn the device back on and restore regular function. Please note that the device is in standby mode and may need a few moments to resume operation. Thank you for your patience and understanding.

What's making the unit beep?

Cooking is underway in both zones: the meal preparation is finished, and the culinary journey is about to begin. Let's get Cooking with a professional touch!

What caused a circuit breaker trip while the unit was being used?

It is essential to ensure that the unit is plugged into a 15-amp outlet when in use, as it requires 1690 watts of electrical power. Plugging the device into a 10-amp breaker will cause the breaker to trip. To avoid this, ensure the device is plugged into an outlet on a 15-amp breaker. Doing so will help prevent the breaker from tripping. As a professional, taking necessary precautions to avoid potential issues is essential.

4-Week Meal Plan

Week 1

Day 1:
Breakfast: Mushrooms Omelet
Lunch: Mozzarella Asparagus
Snack: Cauliflower Rice
Dinner: Smoked Chicken Breast
Dessert: Lava Cake

Day 2:
Breakfast: Italian Kale Frittata
Lunch: Radish Halves
Snack: Cheese Portobello Patties
Dinner: Curry Tender Bites
Dessert: Flax Nutmeg Cookies

Day 3:
Breakfast: Cheeses Crêpes
Lunch: Asparagus with Cheese Slices
Snack: Cheese Cauliflower Bake
Dinner: Garlic Cod Fillets
Dessert: Peppermint Cake

Day 4:
Breakfast: Spinach Egg Florentine
Lunch: Parmesan Grated Courgettes
Snack: Coriander Tofu Cubes
Dinner: Chicken Meatballs
Dessert: Mini Cheesecakes

Day 5:
Breakfast: Peppery Egg Salad
Lunch: Asparagus with Cream Sauce
Snack: Simple-Seasoned Brussels Sprouts
Dinner: Coriander Lamb Sausages
Dessert: Hazelnuts Cookies

Day 6:
Breakfast: Brown Mushroom Muffins
Lunch: Courgette Patties
Snack: Cheddar Courgette Balls
Dinner: Halibut Steaks with Vermouth
Dessert: Almond Chocolate Cookies

Day 7:
Breakfast: Eggs with Sausage
Lunch: Asparagus with Bacon Slices
Snack: Mustard Vegetables Mix
Dinner: Lemon-Seasoned Chicken Thighs
Dessert: Chocolate Brownies

Week 2

Day 1:
Breakfast: Western Eggs with Ham and Cheese
Lunch: Snap Peas Mash in Chicken Stock
Snack: Tasty Mushroom Fritters
Dinner: Lamb Loin with Caraway Seeds
Dessert: Fluffy Chocolate Cake

Day 2:
Breakfast: Egg & Spinach Salad
Lunch: Prosciutto Asparagus Mix
Snack: Super-Easy Keto Risotto
Dinner: Parmesan Fish Fillets
Dessert: Espresso Brownies

Day 3:
Breakfast: Scrambled Egg Muffins
Lunch: Garlicky Fennel Bulb
Snack: Cheddar Broccoli Tots
Dinner: Spiced Chicken Drumsticks
Dessert: Coconut Orange Cake

Day 4:
Breakfast: Porcini Mushrooms Frittata
Lunch: Dijon Asparagus
Snack: Cream Spinach with Chives
Dinner: Butter Rack of Lamb
Dessert: Old-Fashioned Walnut Cookies

Day 5:
Breakfast: Tofu Scramble
Lunch: Cheese Okra
Snack: Healthy Courgette Tots
Dinner: Herbed Prawns
Dessert: Blueberry Cupcakes

Day 6:
Breakfast: Baked Eggs with Sausage
Lunch: Spinach with Chopped Pecan
Snack: Broccoli Hash Brown
Dinner: Flavourful Chicken Wings
Dessert: Lava Cake

Day 7:
Breakfast: Eggs with Spinach & Tomato
Lunch: Okra Bacon Salad
Snack: Aubergine Bites
Dinner: Chopped Beef Oxtails
Dessert: Cranberries Fruitcake

Week 3

Day 1:
Breakfast: Broccoli Bites with Cheese Sauce
Lunch: Cheese Cauliflower Casserole
Snack: Cream Broccoli Puree
Dinner: Lamb Chops with Yogurt
Dessert: Flax Nutmeg Cookies

Day 2:
Breakfast: Mozzarella Sticks with Salsa
Lunch: Kabocha Squash
Snack: Seasoned Brussels Sprouts
Dinner: Coated Chicken Breast
Dessert: Peppermint Cake

Day 3:
Breakfast: Mushrooms Omelet
Lunch: Vinegar Chopped Cauliflower
Snack: Fennel Bulb Wedges
Dinner: Almond Meatballs
Dessert: Mini Cheesecakes

Day 4:
Breakfast: Italian Kale Frittata
Lunch: Cheese Aubergine Mash
Snack: Chopped Tempeh
Dinner: Tuna with Red Onions
Dessert: Hazelnuts Cookies

Day 5:
Breakfast: Cheeses Crêpes
Lunch: Broccoli with Chopped Spring onions
Snack: Cauliflower Rice
Dinner: Salmon Fish Cakes
Dessert: Almond Chocolate Cookies

Day 6:
Breakfast: Spinach Egg Florentine
Lunch: Cheddar Turnip
Snack: Cheese Portobello Patties
Dinner: Rib Eye Steaks
Dessert: Chocolate Brownies

Day 7:
Breakfast: Peppery Egg Salad
Lunch: Mozzarella Asparagus
Snack: Cheese Cauliflower Bake
Dinner: Keto BBQ Wings
Dessert: Fluffy Chocolate Cake

Week 4

Day 1:
Breakfast: Brown Mushroom Muffins
Lunch: Radish Halves
Snack: Coriander Tofu Cubes
Dinner: Easy Turkey Bacon
Dessert: Espresso Brownies

Day 2:
Breakfast: Eggs with Sausage
Lunch: Asparagus with Cheese Slices
Snack: Simple-Seasoned Brussels Sprouts
Dinner: Minced Lamb Sticks
Dessert: Coconut Orange Cake

Day 3:
Breakfast: Western Eggs with Ham and Cheese
Lunch: Parmesan Grated Courgettes
Snack: Cheddar Courgette Balls
Dinner: Tuna Patties
Dessert: Old-Fashioned Walnut Cookies

Day 4:
Breakfast: Egg & Spinach Salad
Lunch: Lamb Burgers
Snack: Mustard Vegetables Mix
Dinner: Clove Lamb Cutlets
Dessert: Blueberry Cupcakes

Day 5:
Breakfast: Scrambled Egg Muffins
Lunch: Courgette Patties
Snack: Tasty Mushroom Fritters
Dinner: Chicken Drumsticks with Jalapeno Peppers
Dessert: Cranberries Fruitcake

Day 6:
Breakfast: Porcini Mushrooms Frittata
Lunch: Asparagus with Bacon Slices
Snack: Super-Easy Keto Risotto
Dinner: Simple Lamb Chops
Dessert: Flax Nutmeg Cookies

Day 7:
Breakfast: Tofu Scramble
Lunch: Snap Peas Mash in Chicken Stock
Snack: Cheddar Broccoli Tots
Dinner: Chicken Wings with Chopped Spinach
Dessert: Peppermint Cake

Chapter 1 Breakfast

Mushrooms Omelet

Prep time: 20 minutes | Cook time: 15 minutes | Serves: 2

1 tablespoon olive oil
80g spring onions, chopped
1 pepper, seeded and thinly sliced
150g button mushrooms, thinly sliced

4 eggs
2 tablespoons milk
Sea salt and freshly ground black pepper, to taste
1 tablespoon fresh chives, for serving

1. Heat the olive oil in a frying pan over medium-high heat; add the spring onions and peppers, and sauté them until aromatic. 2. Add the mushrooms and continue to cook for an additional 3 minutes or until tender. Set aside. 3. Whisk the eggs with milk, salt, and black pepper in a bowl. 4. Insert the crisper plate in the basket in zone 1, and transfer the egg mixture to it. 5. Select AIR FRY mode, adjust the cooking temperature to 180°C and set the cooking time to 7 minutes. 6. Press the START/PAUSE button to begin cooking. 7. Place the reserved mushroom filling on one side of the omelet. Fold your omelet in half and slide onto a serving plate. 8. Serve immediately garnished with fresh chives. Enjoy!
Per Serving: Calories 364; Fat 26.91g; Sodium 221mg; Carbs 9.58g; Fibre 1.9g; Sugar 5.5g; Protein 22g

Italian Kale Frittata

Prep time: 20 minutes | Cook time: 15 minutes | Serves: 3

1 yellow onion, finely chopped
150g wild mushrooms, sliced
6 eggs
60g double cream
½ teaspoon cayenne pepper

Sea salt and ground black pepper, to taste
1 tablespoon butter, melted
2 tablespoons fresh Italian parsley, chopped
60g kale, chopped
60g mozzarella, shredded

1. Insert the crisper plate in the basket in zone 1, and transfer the onions and wild mushrooms to it. 2. Select AIR FRY mode, adjust the cooking temperature to 180°C and set the cooking time to 5 minutes. 3. Press the START/PAUSE button to begin cooking. 4. In a mixing dish, whisk the eggs and double cream until pale. Add the spices, butter, parsley, and kale; stir until everything is well incorporated. 5. Pour the mixture into the basket, top them with the cheese, and resume cooking them for 10 minutes. 6. Serve immediately.
Per Serving: Calories 269; Fat 19.6g; Sodium 316mg; Carbs 8.84g; Fibre 2.2g; Sugar 4.79g; Protein 20.5g

Cheeses Crêpes

Prep time: 35 minutes | Cook time: 6 minutes | Serves: 3

30g coconut flour
1 tablespoon psyllium husk
2 eggs, beaten
3 egg whites, beaten
¼ teaspoon allspice
½ teaspoon salt

1 teaspoon cream of tartar
180ml milk
120g ricotta cheese
50g Parmigiano-Reggiano cheese, preferably freshly grated
240g marinara sauce

1. Mix the coconut flour, psyllium husk, eggs, allspice, salt, and cream of tartar in a large bowl. Gradually add the milk and ricotta cheese and whisk continuously until well combined. 2. Let it stand for 20 minutes. 3. Divide the batter between the baskets in zone 1 and zone 2. 4. Select BAKE mode, adjust the cooking temperature to 110°C and set the cooking time to 6 minutes. 5. Press the MATCH COOK button and copy the zone 1 settings to zone 2. 6. Press the START/PAUSE button to begin cooking. 7. Flip the batter halfway through and then cook until browned in spots. 8. Serve with Parmigiano-Reggiano cheese and marinara sauce.
Per Serving: Calories 245; Fat 14.06g; Sodium 1433mg; Carbs 11.6g; Fibre 1.8g; Sugar 7.53g; Protein 18.72g

Spinach Egg Florentine

Prep time: 20 minutes | Cook time: 12 minutes | Serves: 2

2 tablespoons ghee, melted
60g baby spinach, torn into small pieces
2 tablespoons shallots, chopped
¼ teaspoon red pepper flakes

Salt, to taste
1 tablespoon fresh thyme leaves, roughly chopped
4 eggs

1. Insert the crisper plates in the baskets in zone 1 and zone 2, brush them with the melted ghee; divide the spinach and shallots between them, and season them with red pepper, salt, and fresh thyme. 2. Make four indents for the eggs; crack one egg into each indent. 3. Select BAKE mode, adjust the cooking temperature to 175°C and set the cooking time to 12 minutes. 4. Press the MATCH COOK button and copy the zone 1 settings to zone 2. 5. Press the START/PAUSE button to begin cooking. 6. Flip them once or twice during cooking. 7. When done, serve and enjoy.

Per Serving: Calories 244; Fat 20.08g; Sodium 229mg; Carbs 3.85g; Fibre 1.2g; Sugar 1.27g; Protein 12.38g

Peppery Egg Salad

Prep time: 20 minutes | Cook time: 15 minutes | Serves: 2

6 eggs
1 teaspoon mustard
120g mayonnaise
1 tablespoon white vinegar
1 habanero pepper, minced

1 red pepper, seeded and sliced
1 green pepper, seeded and sliced
1 shallot, sliced
Sea salt and ground black pepper, to taste

1. Insert the crisper plate in the basket in zone 1, and place the eggs in it. 2. Select AIR FRY mode, adjust the cooking temperature to 130°C and set the cooking time to 15 minutes. 3. Press the START/PAUSE button to begin cooking. 4. Transfer them to an ice-cold water bath to stop the cooking. Peel the eggs under cold running water; coarsely chop the hard-boiled eggs and set aside. 5. Toss the eggs with the remaining ingredients and serve well chilled.

Per Serving: Calories 419; Fat 31.94g; Sodium 685mg; Carbs 10.82g; Fibre 2.2g; Sugar 4.94g; Protein 21.81g

Brown Mushroom Muffins

Prep time: 25 minutes | Cook time: 20 minutes | Serves: 6

2 tablespoons butter, melted
1 yellow onion, chopped
2 garlic cloves, minced
100g brown mushrooms, sliced

Sea salt and ground black pepper, to taste
1 teaspoon fresh basil
8 eggs, lightly whisked
150g goat cheese, crumbled

1. Melt the butter in a heavy-bottomed frying pan over medium-high heat. Sauté the onions, garlic, and mushrooms until just tender and fragrant. 2. Add the salt, black pepper, and basil and remove from heat. 3. Spritz a 6-tin muffin tin with cooking spray, and divide out the sautéed mixture into the muffin tin. 4. Pour the whisked eggs on top and top with the goat cheese. 5. Insert the crisper plate in the basket in zone 1, and transfer the muffin tin to it. 6. Select BAKE mode, adjust the cooking temperature to 165°C and set the cooking time to 20 minutes. 7. Press the START/PAUSE button to begin cooking. 8. Enjoy.

Per Serving: Calories 261; Fat 19.57g; Sodium 236mg; Carbs 4.47g; Fibre 0.6g; Sugar 2.26g; Protein 16.87g

Eggs with Sausage

Prep time: 25 minutes | Cook time: 15 minutes | Serves: 6

1 teaspoon lard
225g turkey sausage
6 eggs
1 spring onion, chopped
1 garlic clove, minced

1 pepper, seeded and chopped
1 chili pepper, seeded and chopped
Sea salt and ground black pepper, to taste
50g Swiss cheese, shredded

1. Melt the lard in a saucepan over medium-high heat; add the sausage and cook for 5 minutes or until no longer pink. 2. Coarsely chop the sausage; add the eggs, spring onions, garlic, peppers, salt, and black pepper. 3. Spritz 4 silicone molds with cooking spray. 4. Divide the egg mixture between the silicone molds and top them with the shredded cheese. 5. Transfer the molds to the baskets in the zones. 6. Select BAKE mode, adjust the cooking temperature to 170°C and set the cooking time to 15 minutes. 7. Press the MATCH COOK button and copy the zone 1 settings to zone 2. 8. Press the START/PAUSE button to begin cooking. 9. Serve hot.
Per Serving: Calories 199; Fat 11.9g; Sodium 345mg; Carbs 7.51g; Fibre 0.5g; Sugar 1.52g; Protein 115.44g

Western Eggs with Ham and Cheese

Prep time: 20 minutes | Cook time: 12 minutes | Serves: 4

6 eggs
120ml milk
50g cream cheese, softened
Sea salt, to your liking
¼ teaspoon ground black pepper

¼ teaspoon paprika
150g cooked ham, diced
1 onion, chopped
50g cheddar cheese

1. In a mixing dish, whisk the eggs, milk, and cream cheese until pale. Add the spices, ham, and onion; stir until everything is well incorporated. 2. Pour the mixture into a suitable baking pan; top the mixture with the cheddar cheese. 3. Transfer the pan to the basket in zone 1. 4. Select BAKE mode, adjust the cooking temperature to 180°C and set the cooking time to 12 minutes. 5. Press the START/PAUSE button to begin cooking. 6. Serve warm and enjoy!
Per Serving: Calories 278; Fat 18.41g; Sodium 859mg; Carbs 5.98g; Fibre 0.6g; Sugar 3.65g; Protein 21.79g

Egg & Spinach Salad

Prep time: 25 minutes | Cook time: 20 minutes | Serves: 4

4 eggs
455g asparagus, chopped
60g baby spinach
120g mayonnaise

1 teaspoon mustard
1 teaspoon fresh lemon juice
Sea salt and ground black pepper, to taste

1. Insert the crisper plates in the baskets. 2. Place the eggs in zone 1 and add the asparagus to zone 2. 3. Select AIR FRY mode, adjust the cooking temperature to 130°C and set the cooking time to 15 minutes. 4. Select zone 2, set the AIR FRY mode, and adjust the cooking temperature to 205°C and cooking time to 5 minutes. 5. Press the SMART FINISH button, and then press the START/PAUSE button to begin cooking. 6. Transfer the cooked eggs to an ice-cold water bath to stop the cooking. Peel the eggs under cold running water; coarsely chop the hard-boiled eggs and set aside. 7. Place the cooked asparagus in a salad bowl and add the baby spinach. 8. In a mixing dish, thoroughly combine the remaining ingredients. Drizzle this dressing over the asparagus in the salad bowl and top with the chopped eggs. Enjoy.
Per Serving: Calories 188; Fat 13.98g; Sodium 322mg; Carbs 6.71g; Fibre 3.2g; Sugar 2.66g; Protein 10.35g

Scrambled Egg Muffins

Prep time: 20 minutes | Cook time: 16 minutes | Serves: 6

150g smoked turkey sausage, chopped
6 eggs, lightly beaten
2 tablespoons shallots, finely chopped
2 garlic cloves, minced

Sea salt and ground black pepper, to taste
1 teaspoon cayenne pepper
150g Monterey Jack cheese, shredded

1. Combine the sausage, eggs, shallots, garlic, salt, black pepper, and cayenne pepper in a mixing dish. 2. Spoon the mixture into 6 standard-size muffin cups with paper liners. 3. Transfer the muffin cups into the basket in zone 1. 4. Select BAKE mode, adjust the cooking temperature to 170°C and set the cooking time to 16 minutes. 5. Press the START/PAUSE button to begin cooking. 6. Top the muffins with cheese halfway through the cooking time. 7. Enjoy.
Per Serving: Calories 234; Fat 15.76g; Sodium 438mg; Carbs 5.38g; Fibre 0.4g; Sugar 0.99g; Protein 17.62g

Porcini Mushrooms Frittata

Prep time: 40 minutes | Cook time: 40 minutes | Serves: 4

300g Porcini mushrooms, thinly sliced
1 tablespoon melted butter
1 shallot, peeled and slice into thin rounds
1 garlic cloves, peeled and finely minced
1 lemon grass, cut into 2.5cm pieces
⅓ teaspoon table salt

8 eggs
½ teaspoon ground black pepper, preferably freshly ground
1 teaspoon cumin powder
⅓ teaspoon dried or fresh dill weed
120g goat cheese, crumbled

1. Melt the butter in a nonstick frying pan over medium heat. 2. Sauté the shallot, garlic, thinly sliced Porcini mushrooms and lemon grass over a moderate heat until they have softened. Set them aside. 3. Beat the eggs in a mixing bowl until frothy; add the seasonings and mix to combine well. 4. Divide the egg mixture between the baskets in zone 1 and zone 2, and then onion sauté; top them with the crumbled goat cheese. 5. Select BAKE mode, adjust the cooking temperature to 170°Cand set the cooking time to 32 minutes. 6. Press the MATCH COOK button and copy the zone 1 settings to zone 2. 7. Press the START/PAUSE button to begin cooking. 8. Enjoy.
Per Serving: Calories 224; Fat 16.46g; Sodium 419mg; Carbs 2.69g; Fibre 0.3g; Sugar 1.1g; Protein 15.69g

Tofu Scramble

Prep time: 15 minutes | Cook time: 15 minutes | Serves: 2

½ teaspoon fresh lemon juice
1 teaspoon coarse salt
1 teaspoon coarse ground black pepper
100g fresh spinach, chopped

1 tablespoon butter, melted
15g fresh basil, roughly chopped
½ teaspoon fresh lemon juice
325g soft silken tofu, drained

1. Insert the crisper plate in the basket in zone 1, and transfer the tofu to it; drizzle the tofu with olive oil. 2. Select AIR FRY mode, adjust the cooking temperature to 130°C and set the cooking time to 14 minutes. 3. Press the START/PAUSE button to begin cooking. 4. After 9 minutes of cooking time, add the remaining ingredients to the basket in zone 1 and resume cooking for another 5 minutes. 5. Serve warm.
Per Serving: Calories 181; Fat 12.85g; Sodium 1268mg; Carbs 6.39g; Fibre 2g; Sugar 1.61g; Protein 14.01g

Baked Eggs with Sausage

Prep time: 20 minutes | Cook time: 15 minutes | Serves: 2

50g Cheddar cheese, shredded
4 eggs
50g Linguica (Portuguese pork sausage), chopped
½ onion, peeled and chopped
2 tablespoons olive oil

½ teaspoon rosemary, chopped
½ teaspoon marjoram
60g sour cream
Sea salt and freshly ground black pepper, to taste
½ teaspoon fresh sage, chopped

1. Lightly grease 2 oven-safe ramekins with olive oil, and then divide the sausage and onions between them. 2. Crack an egg into each ramekin; add the remaining items, minus the cheese. 3. Insert the crisper plate in the basket in zone 1, and transfer the ramekins to it. 4. Select AIR FRY mode, adjust the cooking temperature to 180°C and set the cooking time to 13 minutes. 5. Press the START/PAUSE button to begin cooking. 6. When done, top them with the Cheddar cheese and enjoy.
Per Serving: Calories 523; Fat 43.88g; Sodium 594mg; Carbs 6.37g; Fibre 0.6g; Sugar 1.97g; Protein 25.6g

Eggs with Spinach & Tomato

Prep time: 15 minutes | Cook time: 15 minutes | Serves: 2

2 tablespoons olive oil, melted
4 eggs, whisked
125g fresh spinach, chopped
1 medium-sized tomato, chopped

1 teaspoon fresh lemon juice
½ teaspoon coarse salt
½ teaspoon ground black pepper
20g of fresh basil, roughly chopped

1. Simply combine the remaining ingredients, except for the basil leaves; whisk them until everything is well incorporated. 2. Insert the crisper plate in the basket in zone 1, brush it with the olive oil and then transfer the mixture to it. 3. Select AIR FRY mode, adjust the cooking temperature to 140°C and set the cooking time to 12 minutes. 4. Press the START/PAUSE button to begin cooking. 5. When done, garnish the dish with fresh basil leaves. Serve warm with a dollop of sour cream if desired.
Per Serving: Calories 276; Fat 22.33g; Sodium 766mg; Carbs 6.32g; Fibre 2.6g; Sugar 2.33g; Protein 13.88g

Mozzarella Sticks with Salsa

Prep time: 40 minutes | Cook time: 6 minutes | Serves: 4

150g mozzarella cheese strings
2 eggs
2 tablespoons flaxseed meal
25g almond flour

50g parmesan cheese finely grated
1 teaspoon garlic powder
1 teaspoon dried oregano
130g salsa, preferably homemade

1. Put the eggs in a shallow bowl. 2. In another bowl, mix the flaxseed meal, almond flour, parmesan cheese, garlic powder, and oregano. 3. Dip the mozzarella sticks in the egg, and then in the parmesan mixture, and finally in the egg and parmesan mixture again. 4. Place the sticks in your freezer for 30 minutes. 5. Insert the crisper plates in the baskets. Apportion the sticks between the baskets in zone 1 and zone 2. 6. Select AIR FRY mode, adjust the cooking temperature to 190°C and set the cooking time to 6 minutes. 7. Press the MATCH COOK button and copy the zone 1 settings to zone 2. 8. Press the START/PAUSE button to begin cooking. 9. When done, serve the sticks with salsa on the side.
Per Serving: Calories 229; Fat 4.87g; Sodium 1009mg; Carbs 11.56g; Fibre 3.7g; Sugar 2.88g; Protein 35.33g

Broccoli Bites with Cheese Sauce

Prep time: 20 minutes | Cook time: 15 minutes | Serves: 6

For the Broccoli Bites
1 medium-sized head broccoli, broken into florets
½ teaspoon lemon zest, freshly grated
⅓ teaspoon fine sea salt
½ teaspoon hot paprika
1 teaspoon shallot powder

1 teaspoon porcini powder
½ teaspoon granulated garlic
⅓ teaspoon celery seeds
1 ½ tablespoons olive oil

For the Cheese Sauce
2 tablespoons butter
1 tablespoon golden flaxseed meal

240ml milk
110g blue cheese

1. Toss all the ingredients for the broccoli bites in a mixing bowl, covering the broccoli florets on all sides. 2. Insert the crisper plate in the basket in zone 1, and transfer the mixture to it. 3. Select AIR FRY mode, adjust the cooking temperature to 180°C and set the cooking time to 15 minutes. 4. Press the START/PAUSE button to begin cooking. 5. Melt the butter in a saucepan over a medium heat; stir in the golden flaxseed meal and let cook for about 1 minute. 6. Gradually pour in the milk, stirring constantly, until the mixture is smooth. Bring it to a simmer and stir in the cheese and cook until the sauce has thickened slightly. 7. Mix in the cooked broccoli and cook for further 3 minutes. 8. Serve hot.

Per Serving: Calories 141; Fat 12.59g; Sodium 308mg; Carbs 3.41g; Fibre 0.7g; Sugar 2.23g; Protein 4.26g

---

Cod Frittata with Shallot

Prep time: 20 minutes | Cook time: 15 minutes | Serves: 3

2 cod fillets
6 eggs
120ml milk
1 shallot, chopped

2 garlic cloves, minced
Sea salt and ground black pepper, to taste
½ teaspoon red pepper flakes, crushed

1. Bring a pot of salted water to a boil. 2. Boil the cod fillets for 5 minutes or until it is opaque. Flake the fish into bite-sized pieces. 3. In a mixing bowl, whisk the eggs and milk. Stir in the shallots, garlic, salt, black pepper, and red pepper flakes. Stir in the reserved fish. 4. Transfer them to the basket. 5. Select ROAST mode, adjust the cooking temperature to 180°C and set the cooking time to 9 minutes. 6. Press the START/PAUSE button to begin cooking. 7. Flip the food halfway through. 8. Serve hot.

Per Serving: Calories 214; Fat 10.07g; Sodium 378mg; Carbs 5g; Fibre 0.5g; Sugar 3.05g; Protein 24.58g

---

Halibut & Eggs Keto Rolls

Prep time: 25 minutes | Cook time: 20 minutes | Serves: 4

4 keto rolls
455g smoked halibut, chopped
4 eggs

1 teaspoon dried thyme
1 teaspoon dried basil
Salt and black pepper, to taste

1. Cut off the top of each keto roll; then, scoop out the insides to make the shells. 2. Lay two prepared keto roll shells in each basket. 3. Spritz them with cooking oil, add the halibut; crack an egg into each keto roll shell and sprinkle them with the thyme, basil, salt and black pepper. 4. Select ROAST mode, adjust the cooking temperature to 160°C and set the cooking time to 20 minutes. 5. Press the MATCH COOK button and copy the zone 1 settings to zone 2. 6. Press the START/PAUSE button to begin cooking. 7. Serve hot.

Per Serving: Calories 306; Fat 7.6g; Sodium 366mg; Carbs 21.53g; Fibre 1g; Sugar 2.84g; Protein 35.29g

Eggs with Turkey Bacon and Green Onions

Prep time: 25 minutes | Cook time: 25 minutes | Serves: 4

225g turkey bacon
4 eggs
80ml milk
2 tablespoons yogurt

½ teaspoon sea salt
1 pepper, finely chopped
2 green onions, finely chopped
50g cheese, shredded

1. Insert the crisper plates in the baskets. Divide the turkey bacon between the baskets in zone 1 and zone 2. 2. Select AIR FRY mode, adjust the cooking temperature to 180°C and set the cooking time to 11 minutes. 3. Press the MATCH COOK button and copy the zone 1 settings to zone 2. 4. Press the START/PAUSE button to begin cooking. 5. When done, reserve the bacon grease and set them aside. 6. In a mixing bowl, thoroughly whisk the eggs with milk and yogurt. Add salt, pepper, and green onions. 7. Pour the egg mixture in the basket in zone 1. 8. Select AIR FRY mode, adjust the cooking temperature to 180°C and set the cooking time to 11 minutes. 9. Press the START/PAUSE button to begin cooking. 10. Top the egg mixture with the shredded cheese halfway through the cooking time. 11. Serve the scrambled eggs with the reserved bacon!
Per Serving: Calories 286; Fat 20.18g; Sodium 1077mg; Carbs 6.49g; Fibre 0.8g; Sugar 3.58g; Protein 19.95g

Filipino Meat Omelet

Prep time: 20 minutes | Cook time: 15 minutes | Serves: 3

1 teaspoon lard
305g beef mince
¼ teaspoon chili powder
½ teaspoon ground bay leaf
½ teaspoon ground pepper
Sea salt, to taste

1 green pepper, seeded and chopped
1 red pepper, seeded and chopped
6 eggs
80g double cream
50g cheese, shredded
1 tomato, sliced

1. Melt the lard in a frying pan over medium-high heat; add the beef mince and cook for 4 minutes until no longer pink, crumbling with the spatula. 2. In a mixing bowl, whisk the eggs with double cream. 3. Transfer the beef mince to the basket and season them with the chili powder, ground bay leave, salt and ground pepper; top them with the peppers. 4. Spoon the egg mixture over them. 5. Select ROAST mode, adjust the cooking temperature to 180°C and set the cooking time to 15 minutes. 6. Press the START/PAUSE button to begin cooking. 7. After 10 minutes of cooking time, top the dish with cheese and tomato slices, and the resume cooking them until the eggs are golden and the cheese has melted. 8. Serve hot.
Per Serving: Calories 551; Fat 38.51g; Sodium 398mg; Carbs 6g; Fibre 0.7g; Sugar 3.5g; Protein 43.38g

Egg Muffins

Prep time: 20 minutes | Cook time: 15 minutes | Serves: 4

50g almond flour
1 teaspoon baking powder
1 tablespoon granulated sweetener of choice
4 eggs

1 teaspoon cinnamon powder
1 teaspoon vanilla paste
60ml coconut oil
4 tablespoons peanut butter

1. Spritz four silicone muffin tins with cooking spray. 2. Thoroughly combine all ingredients in a mixing dish. Fill the muffin cups with batter. 3. Insert the crisper plate in the basket in zone 1, and transfer the muffin cups to it. 4. Select BAKE mode, adjust the cooking temperature to 165°C and set the cooking time to 13 minutes. 5. Press the START/PAUSE button to begin cooking. 6. Check with a toothpick; when the toothpick comes out clean, the muffins are done. 7. Let the muffins cool for a while before serving.
Per Serving: Calories 244; Fat 20.8g; Sodium 305mg; Carbs 8.19g; Fibre 0.7g; Sugar 5.74g; Protein 6.72g

Mushrooms Steak Pieces with Cheese

Prep time: 25 minutes | Cook time: 20 minutes | Serves: 4

2 eggs, beaten
4 tablespoons yogurt
100g parmesan cheese, grated
1 teaspoon dry mesquite flavoured seasoning mix
Coarse salt and ground black pepper, to taste

½ teaspoon onion powder
455g cube steak, cut into 8 cm long strips
455g button mushrooms
100g Swiss cheese, shredded

1. In a shallow bowl, beat the eggs and yogurt. 2. In a re-sealable bag, mix the parmesan cheese, mesquite seasoning, salt, pepper, and onion powder. 3. Dip the steak pieces in the egg mixture, and transfer them to the bag, and shake to coat on all sides. 4. Divide the steak pieces between the baskets in zone 1 and zone 2. 5. Select BAKE mode, adjust the cooking temperature to 205°C and set the cooking time to 19 minutes. 6. Press the MATCH COOK button and copy the zone 1 settings to zone 2. 7. Press the START/PAUSE button to begin cooking. 8. After 7 minutes of cooking time, flip the beef pieces. 9. After 14 minutes of cooking time, add the mushrooms to the baskets and then resume cooking them for 5 minutes. 10. Serve with the beef nuggets.
Per Serving: Calories 461; Fat 24.7g; Sodium 748mg; Carbs 12.27g; Fibre 1.6g; Sugar 4.6g; Protein 47.75g

Crusted Fish Fingers

Prep time: 20 minutes | Cook time: 15 minutes | Serves: 4

675g tilapia pieces (fingers)
60g coconut flour
2 eggs
1 tablespoon yellow mustard
100g parmesan cheese, grated

1 teaspoon garlic powder
1 teaspoon onion powder
Sea salt and ground black pepper, to taste
½ teaspoon celery powder
2 tablespoons peanut oil

1. Pat the fish fingers dry with a kitchen towel. 2. Place the coconut flour in a shallow dish. 3. In a separate dish, whisk the eggs with mustard. 4. In a third bowl, mix parmesan cheese with the remaining ingredients. 5. Dredge the fish fingers in the flour, shaking the excess into the bowl; dip in the egg mixture and turn to coat evenly; then, dredge in the parmesan mixture, turning a couple of times to coat evenly. 6. Insert the crisper plates in the baskets. Divide the fish fingers between the baskets in zone 1 and zone 2. 7. Select AIR FRY mode, adjust the cooking temperature to 200°C and set the cooking time to 10 minutes. 8. Press the MATCH COOK button and copy the zone 1 settings to zone 2. 9. Press the START/PAUSE button to begin cooking. 10. Turn the fish fingers over halfway through the cooking time. 11. Serve hot.
Per Serving: Calories 374; Fat 18.92g; Sodium 647mg; Carbs 6.39g; Fibre 0.8g; Sugar 0.98g; Protein 44.64g

Homemade Cheese Chips

Prep time: 15 minutes | Cook time: 6 minutes | Serves: 4

100g Parmesan cheese, shredded
100g Cheddar cheese, shredded

1 teaspoon Italian seasoning
120g marinara sauce

1. Mix the cheese with the Italian seasoning. 2. Line the bottom of the baskets with parchment paper. 3. Add about 1 tablespoon of the cheese mixture to each basket, making sure they are not touching. 4. Select BAKE mode, adjust the cooking temperature to 175°C and set the cooking time to 6 minutes. 5. Press the MATCH COOK button and copy the zone 1 settings to zone 2. 6. Press the START/PAUSE button to begin cooking. 7. Place the dish on a large tray to cool slightly. Serve with the marinara sauce.
Per Serving: Calories 258; Fat 18.6g; Sodium 725mg; Carbs 6.93g; Fibre 0.7g; Sugar 1.96g; Protein 15.52g

Onion Rings with Mayo Dip

Prep time: 25 minutes | Cook time: 15 minutes | Serves: 3

1 large onion
50g almond flour
1 teaspoon salt
½ teaspoon ground black pepper
1 teaspoon cayenne pepper
Mayo Dip
3 tablespoons mayonnaise
3 tablespoons sour cream

½ teaspoon dried thyme
½ teaspoon dried oregano
½ teaspoon ground cumin
2 eggs
4 tablespoons milk

1 tablespoon horseradish, drained
Salt and freshly ground black pepper, to taste

1. Cut off the top 1 cm of the Vidalia onion; peel your onion and place it cut-side down. 2. Starting 1 cm from the root, cut the onion in half. Make a second cut that splits each half in two. 3. You will have 4 quarters held together by the root. 4. Repeat these cuts, splitting the 4 quarters to yield eighths; then, you should split them again until you have 16 evenly spaced cuts. 5. Turn the onion over and gently separate the outer pieces. 6. In a mixing bowl, thoroughly combine the almond flour and spices. In a separate bowl, whisk the eggs and milk. 7. Dip the onion rings into the egg mixture, followed by the almond flour mixture. 8. Insert the crisper plates in the baskets. Divide the onion rings between the baskets in zone 1 and zone 2. 9. Select AIR FRY mode, adjust the cooking temperature to 190°C and set the cooking time to 15 minutes. 10. Press the MATCH COOK button and copy the zone 1 settings to zone 2. 11. Press the START/PAUSE button to begin cooking. 12. Whisk the remaining ingredients to make the mayo dip. 13. Serve the onion rings with mayo dip.
Per Serving: Calories 149; Fat 9.88g; Sodium 976mg; Carbs 9.14g; Fibre 1.6g; Sugar 4.26g; Protein 6.59g

Eggs with Pickle Relish

Prep time: 20 minutes | Cook time: 15 minutes | Serves: 3

5 eggs
2 tablespoons mayonnaise
2 tablespoons pickle relish

Sea salt, to taste
½ teaspoon mixed peppercorns, crushed

1. Insert the crisper plate in the basket in zone 1, and transfer the eggs to it. 2. Select AIR FRY mode, adjust the cooking temperature to 130°C and set the cooking time to 15 minutes. 3. Press the START/PAUSE button to begin cooking. 4. Transfer the cooked eggs to an ice-cold water bath to stop the cooking. Peel the eggs under cold running water; slice them into halves. 5. Mash the egg yolks with the mayo, sweet pickle relish, and salt; spoon yolk mixture into egg whites. 6. Arrange on a nice serving platter and garnish with the mixed peppercorns.
Per Serving: Calories 150; Fat 10.2g; Sodium 314mg; Carbs 4.4g; Fibre 0.2g; Sugar 3.29g; Protein 9.84g

Cheddar Pastrami Casserole

Prep time: 20 minutes | Cook time: 10 minutes | Serves: 2

4 eggs
1 pepper, chopped
2 spring onions, chopped
150g pastrami, sliced

60g Greek-style yogurt
50g Cheddar cheese, grated
Sea salt, to taste
¼ teaspoon ground black pepper

1. Thoroughly combine all ingredients and pour the mixture into the basket in zone 1. 2. Select BAKE mode, adjust the cooking temperature to 165°C and set the cooking time to 9 minutes. 3. Press the START/PAUSE button to begin cooking. 4. Place the food on a cooling rack and let it sit for 10 minutes before slicing and serving.
Per Serving: Calories 314; Fat 21.5g; Sodium 593mg; Carbs 6.74g; Fibre 0.8g; Sugar 4.11g; Protein 23.21g

Cheese Sticks with Low-Carb Ketchup

Prep time: 15 minutes | Cook time: 6 minutes | Serves: 4

30g coconut flour
25g almond flour
2 eggs
50g Parmesan cheese, grated

1 tablespoon Cajun seasonings
8 cheese sticks, kid-friendly
60g ketchup, low-carb

1. Place the flour in a shallow dish. 2. In a separate dish, whisk the eggs. 3. Mix the parmesan cheese and Cajun seasoning in a third dish. 4. Dredge the cheese sticks in the flour and then dip in into the egg. Press the cheese sticks into the parmesan mixture, coating them evenly. 5. Insert the crisper plates in the baskets. Divide the cheese sticks between the baskets in zone 1 and zone 2. 6. Select AIR FRY mode, adjust the cooking temperature to 190°C and set the cooking time to 6 minutes. 7. Press the MATCH COOK button and copy the zone 1 settings to zone 2. 8. Press the START/PAUSE button to begin cooking. 9. Serve the cheese sticks with ketchup.
Per Serving: Calories 322; Fat 24.58g; Sodium 799mg; Carbs 4.69g; Fibre 0.5g; Sugar 1.08g; Protein 20g

Italian-Style Broccoli Balls

Prep time: 25 minutes | Cook time: 16 minutes | Serves: 4

225g broccoli
225g Romano cheese, grated
2 garlic cloves, minced
1 shallot, chopped
4 eggs, beaten

2 tablespoons butter, at room temperature
½ teaspoon paprika
¼ teaspoon dried basil
Sea salt and ground black pepper, to taste

1. Add the broccoli to your food processor and pulse until the consistency resembles rice. Stir in the remaining ingredients; mix until everything is well combined. 2. Shape the mixture into bite-sized balls. 3. Insert the crisper plates in the baskets. Divide the balls between the baskets in zone 1 and zone 2. 4. Select AIR FRY mode, adjust the cooking temperature to 190°C and set the cooking time to 16 minutes. 5. Press the MATCH COOK button and copy the zone 1 settings to zone 2. 6. Press the START/PAUSE button to begin cooking. 7. Flip the balls halfway through the cooking time. 8. Serve the dish with cocktail sticks and tomato ketchup on the side.
Per Serving: Calories 351; Fat 25.55g; Sodium 940mg; Carbs 5.11g; Fibre 1.8g; Sugar 1.04g; Protein 25.63g

Japanese Fried Cauliflower Rice

Prep time: 30 minutes | Cook time: 20 minutes | Serves: 2

130g cauliflower rice
2 teaspoons sesame oil
Sea salt and freshly ground black pepper, to your liking
2 eggs, beaten
2 spring onions, white and green parts separated,

chopped
1 tablespoon Shoyu sauce
1 tablespoon sake
2 tablespoons Kewpie Japanese mayonnaise

1. Thoroughly combine the cauliflower rice, sesame oil, salt, and pepper in a bowl. 2. Transfer the cauliflower mixture to the basket. 3. Select ROAST mode, adjust the cooking temperature to 170°C and set the cooking time to 20 minutes. 4. Press the START/PAUSE button to begin cooking. 5. After 7 minutes of cooking time, stir them once. 6. After 13 minutes of cooking time, pour the eggs over them. 7. After 18 minutes of cooking time, add the spring onions and stir them to combine well. 8. Whisk the Shoyu sauce, sake, and Japanese mayonnaise in a mixing bowl. 9. Divide the fried cauliflower rice between individual bowls and serve with the prepared sauce. Enjoy!
Per Serving: Calories 195; Fat 13.8g; Sodium 277mg; Carbs 8.2g; Fibre 2.9g; Sugar 3.04g; Protein 8.93g

Turkey Breast Frittata

Prep time: 50 minutes | Cook time: 45 minutes | Serves: 4

1 tablespoon olive oil
455g turkey breasts, slices
6 large-sized eggs
3 tablespoons Greek yogurt
3 tablespoons Cottage cheese, crumbled

¼ teaspoon ground black pepper
¼ teaspoon red pepper flakes, crushed
Himalayan salt, to taste
1 red pepper, seeded and sliced
1 green pepper, seeded and sliced

1. Insert the crisper plate in the basket in zone 1, and transfer the turkey slices to it. 2. Select AIR FRY mode, adjust the cooking temperature to 175°C and set the cooking time to 30 minutes. 3. Press the START/PAUSE button to begin cooking. 4. Flip the slices halfway through cooking. 5. Cut the cooked turkey slices into bite-sized strips and set aside. 6. Beat the eggs with Greek yogurt, cheese, black pepper, red pepper flakes, and salt. 7. Divide the peppers between the baskets in zone 1 and zone 2, and then the turkey strips and egg mixture. 8. Select BAKE mode, adjust the cooking temperature to 180°C and set the cooking time to 15 minutes. 9. Press the MATCH COOK button and copy the zone 1 settings to zone 2. 10. Press the START/PAUSE button to begin cooking. 11. Serve hot.

Per Serving: Calories 341; Fat 19.03g; Sodium 243mg; Carbs 4.01g; Fibre 0.5g; Sugar 2.55g; Protein 36.51g

Eggs & Seafood Casserole

Prep time: 30 minutes | Cook time: 25 minutes | Serves: 2

1 tablespoon olive oil
2 garlic cloves, minced
1 small yellow onion, chopped
115g tilapia pieces
115g rockfish pieces

½ teaspoon dried basil
Salt and white pepper, to taste
4 eggs, lightly beaten
1 tablespoon dry sherry
4 tablespoons cheese, shredded

1. Heat the olive oil in a frying pan over medium-high heat; add the garlic and onion to the frying pan , and cook them for 2 minutes or until fragrant. 2. In a mixing dish, thoroughly combine the eggs with sherry and cheese. 3. Add the fish basil, salt, pepper, and the onion mixture to the basket in zone 1, and then pour the egg mixture over them. 4. Select ROAST mode, adjust the cooking temperature to 175°C and set the cooking time to 20 minutes. 5. Press the START/PAUSE button to begin cooking. 6. Serve warm.

Per Serving: Calories 414; Fat 23.46g; Sodium 783mg; Carbs 11.66g; Fibre 1.4g; Sugar 7.22g; Protein 38.84g

Chapter 2 Vegetables and Sides

Mozzarella Asparagus

Prep time: 5 minutes | Cook time: 10 minutes | Serves: 4

455g asparagus, roughly chopped
1 teaspoon olive oil

½ teaspoon ground black pepper
50g Parmesan, grated

1. Mix asparagus with olive oil and ground black pepper. 2. Insert the crisper plate in the basket in zone 1, and transfer the asparagus to it. 3. Select AIR FRY mode, adjust the cooking temperature to 205°C and set the cooking time to 10 minutes. 4. Press the START/PAUSE button to begin cooking. 5. After 8 minutes of cooking time, top the asparagus with Parmesan. 6. Serve hot.

Per Serving: Calories 86; Fat 1.98g; Sodium 165mg; Carbs 10.26g; Fibre 2.5g; Sugar 2.35g; Protein8.2g

Radish Halves

Prep time: 10 minutes | Cook time: 5 minutes | Serves: 3

250g radish, halved
1 teaspoon dried rosemary

1 tablespoon coconut oil, melted

1. Mix radish with dried rosemary and coconut oil. 2. Insert the crisper plate in the basket in zone 1, and transfer the radish halves to it. 3. Select ROAST mode, adjust the cooking temperature to 190°C and set the cooking time to 5 minutes. 4. Press the START/PAUSE button to begin cooking. 5. Serve hot.

Per Serving: Calories 52; Fat 4.62g; Sodium 30mg; Carbs 2.68g; Fibre 1.3g; Sugar 1.44g; Protein 0.53g

Asparagus with Cheese Slices

Prep time: 5 minutes | Cook time: 10 minutes | Serves: 4

455g asparagus, trimmed
4 Cheddar cheese slices
1 teaspoon ground paprika

1 teaspoon salt
1 tablespoon avocado oil

1. Mix asparagus with ground paprika, salt, and avocado oil. 2. Cut the cheese slices into the strips. 3. Wrap the asparagus in the cheese. 4. Insert the crisper plate in the basket in zone 1, and transfer the food to it. 5. Select AIR FRY mode, adjust the cooking temperature to 205°C and set the cooking time to 10 minutes. 6. Press the START/ PAUSE button to begin cooking. 7. Serve hot.

Per Serving: Calories 169; Fat 13.18g; Sodium 764mg; Carbs 5.08g; Fibre 2.6g; Sugar 2.27g; Protein 9.31g

Parmesan Grated Courgettes

Prep time: 15 minutes | Cook time: 10 minutes | Serves: 5

2 courgettes, trimmed, grated
75g Parmesan, grated
60g coconut flour

1 teaspoon ground turmeric
1 teaspoon olive oil

1. In the mixing bowl, mix grated courgette with Parmesan, coconut flour, and ground turmeric. 2. Insert the crisper plate in the basket in zone 1, and transfer the food to it. 3. Select AIR FRY mode, adjust the cooking temperature to 185°C and set the cooking time to 10 minutes. 4. Press the START/PAUSE button to begin cooking. 5. Flip them halfway through cooking. 6. Serve hot.

Per Serving: Calories 78; Fat 1.84; Sodium 221mg; Carbs 8.24g; Fibre 0.4g; Sugar 0.9g; Protein 7.16g

Asparagus with Cream Sauce

Prep time: 5 minutes | Cook time: 10 minutes | Serves: 4

455g asparagus, chopped
120g heavy cream
60g mozzarella, shredded

1 teaspoon olive oil
1 teaspoon ground black pepper

1. Sprinkle the asparagus with olive oil and ground black pepper. 2. Insert the crisper plate in the basket in zone 1, and transfer the asparagus to it. 3. Select AIR FRY mode, adjust the cooking temperature to 205°C and set the cooking time to 10 minutes. 4. Press the START/PAUSE button to begin cooking. 5. Mix heavy cream with Mozzarella and bring the liquid to boil. 6. Put the asparagus on the serving plate and top it with cream sauce.
Per Serving: Calories 106; Fat 6.83g; Sodium 113mg; Carbs 5.68g; Fibre 2.8g; Sugar 2.76g; Protein 7.34g

Courgette Patties

Prep time: 15 minutes | Cook time: 6 minutes | Serves: 2

35g Swiss chard, chopped
1 courgette, grated
2 tablespoons almond flour

1 egg, beaten
1 teaspoon olive oil
1 teaspoon salt

1. In the mixing bowl, mix Swiss chard with courgette, almond flour, egg, and salt. 2. Make the patties from the mixture. 3. Insert the crisper plate in the basket in zone 1, and transfer the mixture to it. 4. Select AIR FRY mode, adjust the cooking temperature to 205°C and set the cooking time to 6 minutes. 5. Press the START/PAUSE button to begin cooking. 6. Flip the food halfway through cooking. 7. Serve hot.
Per Serving: Calories 63; Fat 5g; Sodium 1233mg; Carbs 1.26g; Fibre 0.5g; Sugar 0.33g; Protein 3.49g

Asparagus with Bacon Slices

Prep time: 5 minutes | Cook time: 10 minutes | Serves: 4

455g asparagus, trimmed
50g bacon, sliced

1 teaspoon avocado oil
½ teaspoon salt

1. Wrap the asparagus in the bacon slices and sprinkle with avocado oil and salt. 2. Insert the crisper plate in the basket in zone 1, and transfer the asparagus and bacon slices to it. 3. Select AIR FRY mode, adjust the cooking temperature to 205°C and set the cooking time to 10 minutes. 4. Press the START/PAUSE button to begin cooking. 5. Serve hot.
Per Serving: Calories 77; Fat 5.45g; Sodium 501mg; Carbs 5.3g; Fibre 2.7g; Sugar 2.13g; Protein 4.01g

Snap Peas Mash in Chicken Stock

Prep time: 10 minutes | Cook time: 6 minutes | Serves: 4

100g snap peas, frozen
50g Provolone, shredded
1 teaspoon coconut oil

½ teaspoon chili powder
60ml chicken stock

1. Mix snap peas with coconut oil and chicken stock. 2. Transfer the mixture to the basket in zone 1. 3. Select ROAST mode, adjust the cooking temperature to 205°C and set the cooking time to 6 minutes. 4. Press the START/PAUSE button to begin cooking. 5. Transfer the snap peas in the blender, add all remaining ingredients and blend until smooth. Enjoy.
Per Serving: Calories 66; Fat 5.13g; Sodium 156mg; Carbs 1.07g; Fibre 0.1g; Sugar 0.38g; Protein 4.07g

Prosciutto Asparagus Mix

Prep time: 5 minutes | Cook time: 10 minutes | Serves: 4

900g asparagus, trimmed
2 tablespoons avocado oil

120g Mozzarella cheese, shredded
50g prosciutto, chopped

1. Mix asparagus with avocado oil and put in the basket. Top them with mozzarella and prosciutto. 2. Select ROAST mode, adjust the cooking temperature to 205°C and set the cooking time to 10 minutes. 3. Press the START/PAUSE button to begin cooking. 4. Serve hot.
Per Serving: Calories 177; Fat 8.84g; Sodium 222mg; Carbs 9.79g; Fibre 5.3g; Sugar 4.68g; Protein 17.58g

Dijon Asparagus

Prep time: 5 minutes | Cook time: 15 minutes | Serves: 4

455g asparagus, trimmed
2 tablespoons Dijon mustard

1 tablespoon olive oil
1 teaspoon lemon juice

1. In the shallow bowl, mix Dijon mustard with olive oil, and lemon juice. 2. Mix asparagus with mustard mixture. 3. Insert the crisper plate in the basket in zone 1, and transfer the asparagus mixture to it. 4. Select AIR FRY mode, adjust the cooking temperature to 205°C and set the cooking time to 12 minutes. 5. Press the START/PAUSE button to begin cooking. 6. After 10 minutes of cooking time, toss the asparagus. 7. Serve hot.
Per Serving: Calories 57; Fat 3.77g; Sodium 88mg; Carbs 4.94g; Fibre 2.7g; Sugar 2.24g; Protein 2.79g

Okra Bacon Salad

Prep time: 15 minutes | Cook time: 10 minutes | Serves: 4

300g okra, chopped
1 tablespoon avocado oil
1 teaspoon ground turmeric
50g bacon, chopped, roasted

60g lettuce, chopped
1 tablespoon olive oil
1 teaspoon chili flakes

1. Mix okra with avocado oil and ground turmeric. 2. Transfer the okra to the basket. 3. Select ROAST mode, adjust the cooking temperature to 190°C and set the cooking time to 10 minutes. 4. Press the START/PAUSE button to begin cooking. 5. Transfer the okra in the salad bowl, add all remaining ingredients and carefully mix the salad.
Per Serving: Calories 141; Fat 11.4g; Sodium 235mg; Carbs 8.68g; Fibre 3.8g; Sugar 1.59g; Protein 3.69g

Cheese Okra

Prep time: 10 minutes | Cook time: 10 minutes | Serves: 4

455g okra, trimmed
50g Monterey Jack cheese, shredded

1 teaspoon coconut oil, melted
1 teaspoon Italian seasonings

1. Mix okra with coconut oil and Italian seasonings. 2. Insert the crisper plates in the baskets. Divide the okra between the baskets in zone 1 and zone 2. 3. Select AIR FRY mode, adjust the cooking temperature to 190°C and set the cooking time to 10 minutes. 4. Press the MATCH COOK button and copy the zone 1 settings to zone 2. 5. Press the START/PAUSE button to begin cooking. 6. Toss the vegetables and sprinkle them with cheese after 8 minutes of cooking time. 7. Serve hot.
Per Serving: Calories 111; Fat 6.34g; Sodium 159mg; Carbs 8.98g; Fibre 3.7g; Sugar 1.84g; Protein 6.26g

Spinach with Chopped Pecan

Prep time: 5 minutes | Cook time: 12 minutes | Serves: 4

60g fresh spinach, chopped
2 pecans, chopped
1 tablespoon coconut oil

½ teaspoon salt
½ teaspoon ground coriander

1. Mix spinach with coconut oil, salt, and ground coriander. 2. Transfer the food to the basket. 3. Select ROAST mode, adjust the cooking temperature to 175°C and set the cooking time to 12 minutes. 4. Press the START/PAUSE button to begin cooking. 5. Serve hot.
Per Serving: Calories 409; Fat 42.68g; Sodium 303mg; Carbs 8.1g; Fibre 5.6g; Sugar 2.23g; Protein 5.43g

Cheese Cauliflower Casserole

Prep time: 10 minutes | Cook time: 30 minutes | Serves: 4

3 tablespoons coconut oil, melted
240g heavy cream
2 eggs, beaten

200g Monterey Jack cheese, shredded
180g cauliflower, chopped
1 teaspoon dried coriander

1. Mix heavy cream with eggs and pour the liquid over the cheese. 2. Mix cauliflower with coconut oil. 3. Arrange the cauliflower into the baskets in single layer. 4. Top them with coriander and cheese, and pour the egg mixture over them. 5. Select ROAST mode, adjust the cooking temperature to 180°C and set the cooking time to 30 minutes. 6. Press the MATCH COOK button and copy the zone 1 settings to zone 2. 7. Press the START/PAUSE button to begin cooking. 8. Serve hot.
Per Serving: Calories 482; Fat 43.53g; Sodium 455mg; Carbs 4.11g; Fibre 1.1g; Sugar 2.27g; Protein 20.56g

Kabocha Squash

Prep time: 10 minutes | Cook time: 15 minutes | Serves: 4

250g Kabocha squash
1 teaspoon onion powder
25g spring onions, chopped

1 tablespoon olive oil
½ teaspoon chili flakes

1. Cut the squash into cubes and sprinkle with onion powder, olive oil, and chili flakes. 2. Insert the crisper plate in the basket in zone 1, and transfer the squash cubes to it. 3. Select AIR FRY mode, adjust the cooking temperature to 185°Cand set the cooking time to 12 minutes. 4. Press the START/PAUSE button to begin cooking. 5. Toss the cubes halfway through cooking. 6. Top the cooked meal with spring onions.
Per Serving: Calories 63; Fat 3.52g; Sodium 14mg; Carbs 8.55g; Fibre 1.5g; Sugar 0.23g; Protein 0.81g

Garlicky Fennel Bulb

Prep time: 10 minutes | Cook time: 15 minutes | Serves: 2

250g fennel bulb
1 teaspoon avocado oil

1 teaspoon garlic powder

1. Chop the fennel bulb roughly and sprinkle with avocado oil and garlic powder. 2. Insert the crisper plate in the basket in zone 1, and transfer the fennel bulb to it. 3. Select AIR FRY mode, adjust the cooking temperature to 190°C and set the cooking time to 15 minutes. 4. Press the START/PAUSE button to begin cooking. 5. Serve hot.
Per Serving: Calories 69; Fat 2.54g; Sodium 75mg; Carbs 11.48g; Fibre 4.5g; Sugar 5.61g; Protein 2.01g

Vinegar Chopped Cauliflower

Prep time: 5 minutes | Cook time: 25 minutes | Serves: 4

455g cauliflower, chopped
50g spring onions, chopped
½ teaspoon white pepper
100g prosciutto, chopped

1 pecan, chopped
3 tablespoons apple cider vinegar
1 tablespoon avocado oil

1. Mix up all of the ingredients in a bowl. 2. Divide the mixture between the baskets in zone 1 and zone 2. 3. Select ROAST mode, adjust the cooking temperature to 180°C and set the cooking time to 25 minutes. 4. Press the MATCH COOK button and copy the zone 1 settings to zone 2. 5. Press the START/PAUSE button to begin cooking. 6. Serve hot.
Per Serving: Calories 315; Fat 26.58g; Sodium 51mg; Carbs 10.79g; Fibre 5.1g; Sugar 4g; Protein 12.08g

Cheddar Turnip

Prep time: 15 minutes | Cook time: 10 minutes | Serves: 2

150g turnip, chopped
50g Cheddar cheese, grated
1 tablespoon coconut oil
½ teaspoon dried coriander

½ teaspoon salt
½ teaspoon onion powder
3 tablespoons coconut cream

1. Mix turnip with coconut oil, dried coriander, salt, and onion powder. 2. Insert the crisper plate in the basket in zone 1, and transfer the turnip mixture to it, and then top them with coconut cream. 3. Select AIR FRY mode, adjust the cooking temperature to 180°C and set the cooking time to 8 minutes. 4. Press the START/PAUSE button to begin cooking. 5. Flip the turnip halfway through cooking. 6. Top the dish with Cheddar cheese.
Per Serving: Calories 216; Fat 17.26g; Sodium 905mg; Carbs 12.34g; Fibre 2.5g; Sugar 5.84g; Protein 5.6g

Breaded Yellow Squash

Prep time: 20 minutes | Cook time: 12 minutes | Serves: 4

1 large yellow squash
2 eggs
60ml buttermilk
110g panko breadcrumbs

30g polenta
½ teaspoon salt
Oil for misting or cooking spray

1. Cut the squash into ½ cm slices. 2. In a shallow dish, beat together eggs and buttermilk. 3. In sealable plastic bag or container with lid, combine 30 g panko crumbs, polenta, and salt. Shake the bag to mix them well. 4. Place the remaining panko crumbs in a separate shallow dish. 5. Dump all the squash slices into the egg/buttermilk mixture. Stir to coat. 6. Remove squash from buttermilk mixture with a slotted spoon, letting excess drip off, and transfer to the panko mixture. Close bag or container and shake well to coat. 7. Remove squash from crumb mixture, letting excess fall off. Return squash to egg mixture, stirring gently to coat. 8. Remove each squash slice from egg wash and dip in a dish of panko crumbs. 9. Mist squash slices with oil. 10. Insert the crisper plate in the basket in zone 1, and transfer the squash slices to it. 11. Select AIR FRY mode, adjust the cooking temperature to 200°Cand set the cooking time to 10 minutes. 12. Press the START/PAUSE button to begin cooking. 13. Toss the slices and spray them with oil halfway through cooking. 14. If necessary, mist again with oil and cook an additional minute or two, until squash slices are golden brown and crisp. 15. Serve hot.
Per Serving: Calories 198; Fat 4.33g; Sodium 817mg; Carbs 31.7g; Fibre 3.6g; Sugar 5.85g; Protein 8.65g

Homemade Hasselbacks

Prep time: 10 minutes | Cook time: 41 minutes | Serves: 4

2 large potatoes (approx. 455g each)
Oil for misting or cooking spray
Salt, pepper, and garlic powder
35g sharp Cheddar cheese, sliced very thin

40g chopped spring onions
2 strips turkey bacon, cooked and crumbled
Light sour cream for serving (optional)

1. Scrub the potatoes. Cut thin vertical slices ½ cm thick crosswise about three-quarters of the way down so that bottom of potato remains intact. 2. Fan potatoes slightly to separate slices. Mist with oil and sprinkle with salt, pepper, and garlic powder to taste. 3. Insert the crisper plate in the basket in zone 1, and transfer the potatoes to it. 4. Select AIR FRY mode, adjust the cooking temperature to 200°C and set the cooking time to 40 minutes. 5. Press the START/PAUSE button to begin cooking. 6. Top potatoes with cheese slices and cook for 30 seconds to 1 minute to melt cheese. 7. Cut each potato in half crosswise, and sprinkle with green onions and crumbled bacon.
Per Serving: Calories 231; Fat 4.71g; Sodium 135mg; Carbs 40.25g; Fibre 5.1g; Sugar 1.97g; Protein 7.98g

Coated Mushrooms

Prep time: 10 minutes | Cook time: 12 minutes | Serves: 4

200g whole white button mushrooms
½ teaspoon salt
⅛ teaspoon pepper
¼ teaspoon garlic powder
¼ teaspoon onion powder

5 tablespoons potato starch
1 egg, beaten
80g panko breadcrumbs
Oil for misting or cooking spray

1. Place mushrooms in a large bowl. Add the salt, pepper, garlic and onion powders, and stir well to distribute seasonings. 2. Add potato starch to mushrooms and toss in bowl until well coated. 3. Dip mushrooms in beaten egg, roll in panko crumbs, and mist with oil. 4. Insert the crisper plate in the basket in zone 1, and transfer the mushrooms to it. 5. Select AIR FRY mode, adjust the cooking temperature to 200°C and set the cooking time to 12 minutes. 6. Press the START/PAUSE button to begin cooking. 7. Toss the food after 5 minutes of cooking time. 8. When done, the mushrooms should be golden brown and crispy.
Per Serving: Calories 158; Fat 2.43g; Sodium 463mg; Carbs 28.45g; Fibre 3g; Sugar 3.15g; Protein 6.26g

Fingerling Potatoes

Prep time: 5 minutes | Cook time: 20 minutes | Serves: 4

455g fingerling potatoes
1 tablespoon light olive oil
½ teaspoon dried parsley

½ teaspoon lemon juice
Coarsely ground sea salt

1. Cut potatoes in half lengthwise. 2. In a large bowl, coat the potatoes with oil, parsley, and lemon juice. 3. Insert the crisper plates in the baskets. Divide the potatoes between the baskets in zone 1 and zone 2. 4. Select AIR FRY mode, adjust the cooking temperature to 180°C and set the cooking time to 20 minutes. 5. Press the MATCH COOK button and copy the zone 1 settings to zone 2. 6. Press the START/PAUSE button to begin cooking. 7. Sprinkle the dish with sea salt before serving.
Per Serving: Calories 117; Fat 3.48g; Sodium 46mg; Carbs 19.68g; Fibre 2.5g; Sugar 0.9g; Protein 2.3g

Glazed Carrots

Prep time: 10 minutes | Cook time: 10 minutes | Serves: 4

2 teaspoons honey
1 teaspoon orange juice
½ teaspoon grated orange rind
⅛ teaspoon ginger

455g baby carrots
2 teaspoons olive oil
¼ teaspoon salt

1. Combine honey, orange juice, grated rind, and ginger in a small bowl and set aside. 2. Toss the carrots, oil, and salt together to coat well. 3. Insert the crisper plate in the basket in zone 1, and transfer the carrot mixture to it. 4. Select AIR FRY mode, adjust the cooking temperature to 200°C and set the cooking time to 10 minutes. 5. Press the START/PAUSE button to begin cooking. 6. Stir them halfway through cooking. 7. Coat carrots with honey mixture by stirring them, and put them back to the basket in zone 1. 8. Air-fry them at 180°C for 1 minute or just until heated through. 9. Serve hot.
Per Serving: Calories 71; Fat 2.4g; Sodium 234mg; Carbs 12.49g; Fibre 3.3g; Sugar 8.46g; Protein 0.75g

Italian Green Beans

Prep time: 5 minutes | Cook time: 15 minutes | Serves: 4

455g fresh green beans
2 tablespoons Italian salad dressing

Salt and pepper

1. Wash beans and snap off stem ends. 2. In a large bowl, toss beans with Italian dressing. 3. Insert the crisper plate in the basket in zone 1, and transfer the beans to it. 4. Select AIR FRY mode, adjust the cooking temperature to 165°C and set the cooking time to 15 minutes. 5. Press the START/PAUSE button to begin cooking. 6. Stir the beans every 5 minutes during cooking. 7. When cooked, beans should shrivel slightly and brown in places. 8. Sprinkle the dish with salt and pepper to taste.
Per Serving: Calories 72; Fat 5.69g; Sodium 46mg; Carbs 4.95g; Fibre 2.2g; Sugar 0.92g; Protein 1.34g

Mashed Sweet Potato Tots

Prep time: 10 minutes | Cook time: 13 minutes | Serves: 4-6

225g cooked mashed sweet potatoes
1 egg white, beaten
⅛ teaspoon ground cinnamon
1 dash nutmeg
2 tablespoons chopped pecans

1½ teaspoons honey
Salt
55g panko breadcrumbs
Oil for misting or cooking spray

1. In a large bowl, mix together the potatoes, egg white, cinnamon, nutmeg, pecans, honey, and salt to taste. 2. Place panko crumbs on a sheet of wax paper. 3. For each tot, use about 2 teaspoons of sweet potato mixture. 4. To shape, drop the measure of potato mixture onto panko crumbs and push crumbs up and around potatoes to coat edges. Then turn tot over to coat other side with crumbs. 5. Mist tots with oil. 6. Insert the crisper plates in the baskets. Divide the batter between the baskets in zone 1 and zone 2. 7. Select AIR FRY mode, adjust the cooking temperature to 200°C and set the cooking time to 13 minutes. 8. Press the MATCH COOK button and copy the zone 1 settings to zone 2. 9. Press the START/PAUSE button to begin cooking.
Per Serving: Calories 104; Fat 2.43g; Sodium 125mg; Carbs 18.18g; Fibre 2.1g; Sugar 5.29g; Protein 2.79g

Cheese Aubergine Mash

Prep time: 10 minutes | Cook time: 20 minutes | Serves: 6

300g aubergines, peeled
1 tablespoon coconut oil
1 garlic clove, minced

25g Parmesan, grated
1 tablespoon cream cheese

1. Chop the aubergines roughly and sprinkle them with coconut oil. 2. Insert the crisper plates in the baskets. Divide the aubergines between the baskets in zone 1 and zone 2. 3. Select BAKE mode, adjust the cooking temperature to 175°C and set the cooking time to 20 minutes. 4. Press the MATCH COOK button and copy the zone 1 settings to zone 2. 5. Press the START/PAUSE button to begin cooking. 6. Transfer the cooked aubergines in the blender. Add all remaining ingredients and blend the mixture until smooth. Enjoy.
Per Serving: Calories 59; Fat 3.32g; Sodium 67mg; Carbs 5.48g; Fibre 1.7g; Sugar 2.17g; Protein 2.66g

Broccoli with Chopped Spring onions

Prep time: 5 minutes | Cook time: 15 minutes | Serves: 4

455g broccoli, roughly chopped
1 tablespoon olive oil

1 teaspoon salt
50g spring onions, chopped

1. Mix broccoli with olive oil and salt. 2. Insert the crisper plate in the basket in zone 1, and transfer the mixture to it. 3. Select AIR FRY mode, adjust the cooking temperature to 185°C and set the cooking time to 15 minutes. 4. Press the START/PAUSE button to begin cooking. 5. Flip them after 5 minutes of cooking time. 6. After 10 minutes of cooking time, sprinkle the broccoli with spring onions. 7. Serve hot.
Per Serving: Calories 59; Fat 3.96g; Sodium 621mg; Carbs 4.27g; Fibre 3.4g; Sugar 0.76g; Protein 3.85g

Curried Fruit

Prep time: 10 minutes | Cook time: 20 minutes | Serves: 6-8

210g cubed fresh pineapple
120g cubed fresh pear (firm, not overly ripe)
200g frozen peaches, thawed

1 (375g) can dark, sweet, pitted cherries with juice
2 tablespoons brown sugar
1 teaspoon curry powder

1. Combine all ingredients in large bowl. Stir them gently to mix in the sugar and curry. 2. Transfer the food to the basket in zone 1. 3. Select BAKE mode, adjust the cooking temperature to 180°C and set the cooking time to 20 minutes. 4. Press the START/PAUSE button to begin cooking. 5. Stir fruit halfway through cooking. 6. Serve hot.
Per Serving: Calories 107; Fat 0.15g; Sodium 5mg; Carbs 27.54g; Fibre 2.2g; Sugar 24.35g; Protein 0.9g

Green Peas with Shredded Lettuce

Prep time: 5 minutes | Cook time: 5 minutes | Serves: 4

30g shredded lettuce
1 (250g) package frozen green peas, thawed

1 tablespoon fresh mint, shredded
1 teaspoon melted butter

1. Lay the shredded lettuce in the basket. 2. Toss together the peas, mint, and melted butter and spoon over the lettuce. 3. Select ROAST mode, adjust the cooking temperature to 180°C and set the cooking time to 5 minutes. 4. Press the START/PAUSE button to begin cooking. 5. Serve the warm peas and wilted lettuce.
Per Serving: Calories 48; Fat 1.49g; Sodium 75mg; Carbs 6.05g; Fibre 2g; Sugar 2.23g; Protein 2.85g

Roasted Sweet Potatoes

Prep time: 10 minutes | Cook time: 15 minutes | Serves: 4

½ teaspoon ground cinnamon
¼ teaspoon ground cumin
¼ teaspoon paprika
1 teaspoon chili powder
⅛ teaspoon turmeric

½ teaspoon salt (optional)
Freshly ground black pepper
2 large sweet potatoes, peeled and cut into 1.5cm – 2cm
1 tablespoon olive oil

1. In a large bowl, mix together cinnamon, cumin, paprika, chili powder, turmeric, salt, and pepper to taste. 2. Add potatoes and stir well. 3. Drizzle the seasoned potatoes with the olive oil and stir until evenly coated. 4. Insert the crisper plate in the basket in zone 1, and transfer the potatoes to it. 5. Select ROAST mode, adjust the cooking temperature to 200°C and set the cooking time to 12 minutes. 6. Stir the potatoes halfway through cooking.
Per Serving: Calories 116; Fat 3.68g; Sodium 343mg; Carbs 19.81g; Fibre 3.6g; Sugar 5.91g; Protein 2.03g

Mashed Potato Tots

Prep time: 20 minutes | Cook time: 12 minutes | Serves: 4-6

250g cooked mashed potatoes
1 tablespoon bacon bits
2 tablespoons chopped green onions, tops only
¼ teaspoon onion powder
1 teaspoon dried chopped chives

Salt
2 tablespoons flour
1 egg white, beaten
55g panko breadcrumbs
Oil for misting or cooking spray

1. In a large bowl, mix together the potatoes, bacon bits, onions, onion powder, chives, salt to taste, and flour. Add egg white and stir well. 2. Place panko crumbs on a sheet of wax paper. 3. For each tot, use about 2 teaspoons of potato mixture. 4. To shape, drop the measure of potato mixture onto panko crumbs and push crumbs up and around potatoes to coat edges. Then turn tot over to coat other side with crumbs. 5. Insert the crisper plates in the baskets. Divide the tots between the baskets in zone 1 and zone 2, and spray them with oil. 6. Select AIR FRY mode, adjust the cooking temperature to 200°C and set the cooking time to 12 minutes. 7. Press the MATCH COOK button and copy the zone 1 settings to zone 2. 8. Press the START/PAUSE button to begin cooking. 9. Serve hot.
Per Serving: Calories 42; Fat 0.38g; Sodium 59mg; Carbs 7.89g; Fibre 0.7g; Sugar 0.37g; Protein 1.75g

Hawaiian Brown Rice with Sausage

Prep time: 10 minutes | Cook time: 16 minutes | Serves: 4-6

115g sausage meat
1 teaspoon butter
40g minced onion

35g minced pepper
400g cooked brown rice
1 (200g) can crushed pineapple, drained

1. Shape sausage into 3 or 4 thin patties. 2. Insert the crisper plate in the basket in zone 1, and transfer the sausage slices to it. 3. Select AIR FRY mode, adjust the cooking temperature to 200°C and set the cooking time to 8 minutes. 4. Press the START/PAUSE button to begin cooking. 5. When done, remove the sausage patties, drain, and crumble them. Set aside. 6. Add butter, onion, and pepper to the basket in zone 2; bake them at 200°C for 5 minutes or just until vegetables are tender. 7. Add sausage, rice, and pineapple to vegetables and stir together. 8. Bake them at 200°C for 2 to 3 minutes longer. 9. Serve hot.
Per Serving: Calories 176; Fat 2.71g; Sodium 21mg; Carbs 32.3g; Fibre 1.5g; Sugar 17.01g; Protein 5.98g

Potato Cubes

Prep time: 10 minutes | Cook time: 25 minutes | Serves: 3-4

1.3kg potatoes cut into 2.5cm cubes
½ teaspoon oil

Salt and pepper

1. In a large bowl, mix the potatoes and oil thoroughly. 2. Insert the crisper plate in the basket in zone 1, and transfer the potatoes to it. 3. Select AIR FRY mode, adjust the cooking temperature to 200°C and set the cooking time to 25 minutes. 4. Press the START/PAUSE button to begin cooking. 5. Toss the potato cubes after 10 minutes of cooking time. 6. When cooked, season the potato cubes with salt and pepper. Enjoy.
Per Serving: Calories 267; Fat 0.88g; Sodium 20mg; Carbs 59.45g; Fibre 7.5g; Sugar 2.65g; Protein 6.87g

Breaded Okra

Prep time: 15 minutes | Cook time: 17 minutes | Serves: 4

200g fresh okra
1 egg
240ml milk

100g breadcrumbs
½ teaspoon salt
Oil for misting or cooking spray

1. Remove stem ends from okra and cut in 1 cm slices. 2. In a medium bowl, beat together egg and milk. Add okra slices and stir to coat. 3. In a sealable plastic bag or container with lid, mix together the breadcrumbs and salt. 4. Remove okra from egg mixture, letting excess drip off, and transfer into bag with breadcrumbs. 5. Shake okra in crumbs to coat well. 6. Insert the crisper plate in the basket in zone 1, and transfer the okra to it, and spray them with oil. 7. Select AIR FRY mode, adjust the cooking temperature to 200°C and set the cooking time to 15 minutes. 8. Press the START/PAUSE button to begin cooking. 9. Toss the food and spray them with oil every 5 minutes. 10. Serve hot.
Per Serving: Calories 176; Fat 4.57g; Sodium 534mg; Carbs 26.13g; Fibre 2.8g; Sugar 5.53g; Protein 7.87g

Breaded Onion Rings

Prep time: 15 minutes | Cook time: 16 minutes | Serves: 4

1 large onion
65g flour, plus 2 tablespoons
½ teaspoon salt

120ml beer, plus 2 tablespoons
110g crushed panko breadcrumbs
Oil for misting or cooking spray

1. Peel onion, slice, and separate into rings. 2. In a large bowl, mix together the flour and salt. Add beer and stir until it stops foaming and makes a thick batter. 3. Place onion rings in batter and stir to coat. 4. Place breadcrumbs in a sealable plastic bag or container with lid. 5. Working with a few at a time, remove onion rings from batter, shaking off excess, and drop into breadcrumbs. Shake to coat, and then lay out onion rings on cookie sheet or wax paper. 6. When finished, spray onion rings with oil. 7. Insert the crisper plate in the basket in zone 1, and pile the onion rings on it. 8. Select AIR FRY mode, adjust the cooking temperature to 200°C and set the cooking time to 15 minutes. 9. Press the START/PAUSE button to begin cooking. 10. Toss the food and spray them with oil every 5 minutes. 11. Serve hot.
Per Serving: Calories 237; Fat 6.33g; Sodium 581mg; Carbs 36.78g; Fibre 2.4g; Sugar 3.56g; Protein 7.6g

Seasoned Onions

Prep time: 10 minutes | Cook time: 20 minutes | Serves: 4

2 yellow onions
Salt and pepper
¼ teaspoon ground thyme

¼ teaspoon smoked paprika
2 teaspoons olive oil
25g Gruyère cheese, grated

1. Peel onions and halve lengthwise. 2. Sprinkle the cut-side of onions with salt, pepper, thyme, and paprika. 3. Place each onion half, cut-surface up, on a large square of aluminum foil. Pull sides of foil up to cup around onion. Drizzle cut surface of onions with oil. 4. Crimp foil at top to seal closed. 5. Insert the crisper plate in the basket in zone 1, and transfer the wrapped onions to it. 6. Select AIR FRY mode, adjust the cooking temperature to 200°C and set the cooking time to 20 minutes. 7. Press the START/PAUSE button to begin cooking. 8. When done, onions should be soft enough to pierce with fork but still slightly firm. 9. Open the foil just enough to sprinkle each onion with grated cheese, and then cook them for 30 seconds to 1 minute to melt cheese. 10. Enjoy.
Per Serving: Calories 46; Fat 3.81g; Sodium 159mg; Carbs 1.83g; Fibre 0.3g; Sugar 1.34g; Protein 1.36g

---

Polenta

Prep time: 5 minutes | Cook time: 15 minutes | Serves: 4

455g polenta
30g flour

Oil for misting or cooking spray

1. Cut polenta into 1 cm slices. 2. Dip slices in flour to coat well. Spray both sides with oil or cooking spray. 3. Insert the crisper plate in the basket in zone 1, and transfer the polenta slices to it. 4. Select AIR FRY mode, adjust the cooking temperature to 200°C and set the cooking time to 15 minutes. 5. Press the START/PAUSE button to begin cooking. 6. Turn the slices over and spray both sides with oil after 5 minutes of cooking time. 7. Serve the crispy polenta slices.
Per Serving: Calories 135; Fat 0.58g; Sodium 252mg; Carbs 28.81g; Fibre 1.3g; Sugar 0.49g; Protein 2.85g

---

Rosemary Potatoes

Prep time: 10 minutes | Cook time: 6 minutes | Serves: 4

3 large red potatoes
¼ teaspoon ground rosemary
¼ teaspoon ground thyme

⅛ teaspoon salt
⅛ teaspoon ground black pepper
2 teaspoons extra-light olive oil

1. Place potatoes in large bowl and sprinkle them with rosemary, thyme, salt, and pepper, stir them to coat the potatoes well. 2. Coat the potatoes with oil. 3. Insert the crisper plates in the baskets. Divide the potatoes between the baskets in zone 1 and zone 2. 4. Select AIR FRY mode, adjust the cooking temperature to 165°C and set the cooking time to 6 minutes. 5. Press the MATCH COOK button and copy the zone 1 settings to zone 2. 6. Press the START/PAUSE button to begin cooking. 7. Stir the potatoes after 4 minutes of cooking time. 8. Serve hot.
Per Serving: Calories 214; Fat 2.64g; Sodium 127mg; Carbs 44.17g; Fibre 4.7g; Sugar 3.65g; Protein 5.26g

Marjoram Sweet Potato Fries

Prep time: 15 minutes | Cook time: 30 minutes | Serves: 4

900g sweet potatoes
1 teaspoon dried marjoram

2 teaspoons olive oil
Sea salt

1. Peel and cut the potatoes into ½ cm sticks, 10 to 12 cm long. 2. In a sealable plastic bag or bowl with lid, toss sweet potatoes with marjoram and olive oil. Rub seasonings in to coat well. 3. Insert the crisper plate in the basket in zone 1, and transfer the sweet potatoes to it. 4. Select AIR FRY mode, adjust the cooking temperature to 200°C and set the cooking time to 30 minutes. 5. Press the START/PAUSE button to begin cooking. 6. There will be some brown spots on edges when cooked. 7. Season the food with sea salt before serving.
Per Serving: Calories 195; Fat 2.46g; Sodium 53mg; Carbs 39.71g; Fibre 5.1g; Sugar 1.78g; Protein 4.6g

Homemade French Fries

Prep time: 15 minutes | Cook time: 25 minutes | Serves: 4

280g fresh potatoes
2 teaspoons oil

½ teaspoon salt

1. Cut potatoes into 1 cm-wide slices, then lay slices flat and cut into 1 cm sticks. 2. Rinse potato sticks and blot dry with a clean towel. 3. In a bowl or sealable plastic bag, mix the potatoes, oil, and salt together. 4. Insert the crisper plate in the basket in zone 1, and transfer the potato slices to it. 5. Select AIR FRY mode, adjust the cooking temperature to 200°C and set the cooking time to 25 minutes. 6. Press the START/PAUSE button to begin cooking. 7. Stir the food after 10 minutes of cooking time. 8. When done, the fries should be golden brown.
Per Serving: Calories 78; Fat 2.32g; Sodium 295mg; Carbs 13.1g; Fibre 1.7g; Sugar 0.59g; Protein 1.52g

Seasoned White Mushrooms

Prep time: 1-5 minutes | Cook time: 1-5 minutes | Serves: 2-4

200g sliced white mushrooms, rinsed and well drained
¼ teaspoon garlic powder

1 tablespoon Worcestershire sauce

1. Place mushrooms in a large bowl and sprinkle with garlic powder and Worcestershire. Stir well to distribute seasonings evenly. 2. Insert the crisper plate in the basket in zone 1, and transfer the mushrooms to it. 3. Select AIR FRY mode, adjust the cooking temperature to 180°C and set the cooking time to 7 minutes. 4. Press the START/PAUSE button to begin cooking. 5. Serve hot.
Per Serving: Calories 16; Fat 0.19g; Sodium 45mg; Carbs 2.82g; Fibre 0.6g; Sugar 1.55g; Protein 1.79g

Smoked Chicken Breast

Prep time: 10 minutes | Cook time: 20 minutes | Serves: 4

900g chicken breast, skinless, boneless
1 tablespoon smoked paprika

1 teaspoon coconut oil, melted
1 tablespoon apple cider vinegar

1. In the shallow bowl, mix coconut oil with apple cider vinegar, and smoked paprika. 2. Carefully brush the chicken breast with smoked paprika mixture. 3. Insert the crisper plate in the basket in zone 1, and transfer the chicken breast to it. 4. Select AIR FRY mode, adjust the cooking temperature to 190°C and set the cooking time to 20 minutes. 5. Press the START/PAUSE button to begin cooking. 6. Flip the food halfway through cooking. 7. Serve hot.

Per Serving: Calories 405; Fat 22.32g; Sodium 144mg; Carbs 0.95g; Fibre 0.6g; Sugar 0.19g; Protein 47.53g

---

Chicken Meatballs

Prep time: 10 minutes | Cook time: 15 minutes | Serves: 6

400g chicken mince
50g almond flour
1 teaspoon salt

1 teaspoon ground black pepper
1 tablespoon avocado oil

1. Mix chicken mince with almond flour, salt, and ground black pepper. 2. Form the mixture into balls. 3. Insert the crisper plates in the baskets. Divide the meatballs between the baskets in zone 1 and zone 2, and spray them with avocado oil. 4. Select AIR FRY mode, adjust the cooking temperature to 190°C and set the cooking time to 12 minutes. 5. Press the MATCH COOK button and copy the zone 1 settings to zone 2. 6. Press the START/PAUSE button to begin cooking. 7. Serve hot.

Per Serving: Calories 131; Fat 8.52g; Sodium 433mg; Carbs 0.36g; Fibre 0.1g; Sugar 0.01g; Protein 13.26g

---

Lemon–Seasoned Chicken Thighs

Prep time: 5 minutes | Cook time: 30 minutes | Serves: 4

8 chicken thighs, boneless, skinless
1 tablespoon lemon zest, grated
2 tablespoons lemon juice

1 teaspoon avocado oil
1 teaspoon salt

1. Rub the chicken thighs with lemon zest, lemon juice, avocado oil, and salt. 2. Insert the crisper plate in the basket in zone 1, and transfer the chicken thighs to it. 3. Select AIR FRY mode, adjust the cooking temperature to 190°C and set the cooking time to 45 minutes. 4. Press the START/PAUSE button to begin cooking. 5. Flip the chicken thighs after 30 minutes of cooking time. 6. Serve hot.

Per Serving: Calories 470; Fat 16.73g; Sodium 941mg; Carbs 0.79g; Fibre 0g; Sugar 0.29g; Protein 74.35g

---

Flavourful Chicken Wings

Prep time: 10 minutes | Cook time: 30 minutes | Serves: 4

900g of chicken wings
1 tablespoon coconut oil, softened

1 tablespoon garlic powder
60ml apple cider vinegar

1. Mix chicken wings with coconut oil, garlic powder, and apple cider vinegar. 2. Insert the crisper plate in the basket in zone 1, and transfer the chicken wings to it. 3. Select AIR FRY mode, adjust the cooking temperature to 185°C and set the cooking time to 30 minutes. 4. Press the START/PAUSE button to begin cooking. 5. Serve hot.

Per Serving: Calories 330; Fat 11.46g; Sodium 186mg; Carbs 3.52g; Fibre 0.2g; Sugar 1.55g; Protein 50.24g

Spiced Chicken Drumsticks

Prep time: 10 minutes | Cook time: 20 minutes | Serves: 6

6 chicken drumsticks
1 tablespoon coconut oil, melted
1 tablespoon ground coriander

1 teaspoon garlic powder
½ teaspoon salt

1. Sprinkle the chicken drumsticks with ground coriander, salt, and garlic powder. 2. Sprinkle the chicken drumsticks with coconut oil. 3. Insert the crisper plates in the baskets. Divide the chicken drumsticks between the baskets in zone 1 and zone 2. 4. Select AIR FRY mode, adjust the cooking temperature to 190°C and set the cooking time to 20 minutes. 5. Press the MATCH COOK button and copy the zone 1 settings to zone 2. 6. Press the START/PAUSE button to begin cooking. 7. Serve hot.
Per Serving: Calories 231; Fat 14.23g; Sodium 332mg; Carbs 0.52g; Fibre 0.1g; Sugar 0.01g; Protein 23.59g

Sweet Chicken Wings

Prep time: 10 minutes | Cook time: 16 minutes | Serves: 4

455g chicken wings
1 tablespoon taco seasonings

1 tablespoon Erythritol
1 tablespoon coconut oil, melted

1. Mix chicken wings with taco seasonings, Erythritol, and coconut oil. 2. Insert the crisper plate in the basket in zone 1, and transfer the chicken wings to it. 3. Select AIR FRY mode, adjust the cooking temperature to 190°C and set the cooking time to 16 minutes. 4. Press the START/PAUSE button to begin cooking. 5. Serve warm.
Per Serving: Calories 231; Fat 10.92g; Sodium 248mg; Carbs 7.44g; Fibre 0.8g; Sugar 5.51g; Protein 25.41g

Basil Chicken Wings

Prep time: 5 minutes | Cook time: 30 minutes | Serves: 4

900g of chicken wings
1 tablespoon dried basil

1 teaspoon salt
1 tablespoon avocado oil

1. Coat the chicken wings with dried basil, salt, and avocado oil. 2. Insert the crisper plate in the basket in zone 1, and transfer the chicken wings to it. 3. Select AIR FRY mode, adjust the cooking temperature to 180°C and set the cooking time to 30 minutes. 4. Press the START/PAUSE button to begin cooking. 5. Serve warm.
Per Serving: Calories 317; Fat 11.53g; Sodium 765mg; Carbs 0.02g; Fibre 0g; Sugar 0g; Protein 49.85g

Coated Chicken Breast

Prep time: 15 minutes | Cook time: 20 minutes | Serves: 6

1.3kg chicken breast, skinless, boneless
1 tablespoon coconut shred
2 tablespoons parmesan cheese

1 teaspoon ground black pepper
2 eggs, beaten
1 tablespoon avocado oil

1. In the shallow bowl, mix coconut shred with parmesan cheese, and ground black pepper. 2. Cut the chicken breasts into 6 servings and dip in the eggs. 3. Coat the chicken in the coconut shred mixture. 4. Insert the crisper plates in the baskets. Divide the chicken breasts between the baskets in zone 1 and zone 2, and spray them with avocado oil. 5. Select AIR FRY mode, adjust the cooking temperature to 190°C and set the cooking time to 20 minutes. 6. Press the MATCH COOK button and copy the zone 1 settings to zone 2. 7. Press the START/PAUSE button to begin cooking. 8. Serve warm.
Per Serving: Calories 460; Fat 26.7g; Sodium 181mg; Carbs 0.75g; Fibre 0.1g; Sugar 0.29g; Protein 51.06g

Gingered Chicken Drumsticks

Prep time: 5 minutes | Cook time: 20 minutes | Serves: 4

1 teaspoon ground ginger
½ teaspoon ground cinnamon
1 tablespoon olive oil

½ teaspoon onion powder
900g chicken drumsticks

1. Coat the chicken drumsticks with onion powder, olive oil, ground cinnamon, and ground ginger. 2. Insert the crisper plates in the baskets. Divide the chicken drumsticks between the baskets in zone 1 and zone 2. 3. Select AIR FRY mode, adjust the cooking temperature to 190°C and set the cooking time to 20 minutes. 4. Press the MATCH COOK button and copy the zone 1 settings to zone 2. 5. Press the START/PAUSE button to begin cooking. 6. Serve hot.

Per Serving: Calories 398; Fat 24.27g; Sodium 241mg; Carbs 1.07g; Fibre 0.3g; Sugar 0.04g; Protein 41.09g

Keto BBQ Wings

Prep time: 10 minutes | Cook time: 20 minutes | Serves: 4

900g chicken wings
240g keto BBQ sauce

1 teaspoon olive oil

1. Mix the chicken wings with BBQ sauce and olive oil. 2. Insert the crisper plate in the basket in zone 1, and transfer the chicken wings to it. 3. Select AIR FRY mode, adjust the cooking temperature to 190°C and set the cooking time to 18 minutes. 4. Press the START/PAUSE button to begin cooking. 5. Cook the chicken wings for 9 minutes on each side.

Per Serving: Calories 315; Fat 9.26g; Sodium 642mg; Carbs 4.37g; Fibre 1.2g; Sugar 2.56g; Protein 50.83g

Asparagus Chicken Thighs

Prep time: 15 minutes | Cook time: 25 minutes | Serves: 4

95g asparagus, chopped
455g chicken thighs, skinless, boneless
1 teaspoon onion powder

25g spring onions, chopped
1 tablespoon coconut oil, melted
1 teaspoon smoked paprika

1. Mix chicken thighs with onion powder, coconut oil, and smoked paprika. 2. Insert the crisper plate in the basket in zone 1, and transfer the chicken thighs to it. 3. Select AIR FRY mode, adjust the cooking temperature to 195°C and set the cooking time to 25 minutes. 4. Press the START/PAUSE button to begin cooking. 5. Flip the chicken thighs and top them with the chopped asparagus and spring onions after 20 minutes of cooking time.

Per Serving: Calories 293; Fat 22.37g; Sodium 94mg; Carbs 2.89g; Fibre 1.2g; Sugar 0.89g; Protein 19.74g

Simple–Spiced Chicken Fillets

Prep time: 15 minutes | Cook time: 12 minutes | Serves: 4

400g chicken fillets
1 teaspoon ground nutmeg

1 tablespoon avocado oil
½ teaspoon salt

1. Mix the ground nutmeg, avocado oil and salt. 2. Rub the chicken fillet with a nutmeg mixture. 3. Insert the crisper plates in the baskets. Divide the chicken fillets between the baskets in zone 1 and zone 2. 4. Select AIR FRY mode, adjust the cooking temperature to 195°C and set the cooking time to 12 minutes. 5. Press the MATCH COOK button and copy the zone 1 settings to zone 2. 6. Press the START/PAUSE button to begin cooking.

Per Serving: Calories 196; Fat 12.89g; Sodium 359mg; Carbs 0.32g; Fibre 0.1g; Sugar 0.02g; Protein 19.81g

Chicken Thighs with Kalamata Olive Slices

Prep time: 10 minutes | Cook time: 30 minutes | Serves: 4

8 chicken thighs, boneless, skinless
1 tablespoon coconut oil, melted
1 teaspoon dried basil

½ teaspoon cumin seeds
4 kalamata olives, sliced

1. Rub the chicken thighs with coconut oil, dried basil, and cumin seeds. 2. Insert the crisper plates in the baskets. 3. Divide the chicken thighs between the baskets in zone 1 and zone 2. 4. Select ROAST mode, adjust the cooking temperature to 190°C and set the cooking time to 30 minutes. 5. Press the MATCH COOK button and copy the zone 1 settings to zone 2. 6. Press the START/PAUSE button to begin cooking. 7. Flip the chicken thighs and top them with the kalamata olives after 20 minutes of cooking time.
Per Serving: Calories 502; Fat 19.79g; Sodium 409mg; Carbs 0.31g; Fibre 0.2g; Sugar 0.02g; Protein 76g

Taco Chicken

Prep time: 15 minutes | Cook time: 30 minutes | Serves: 4

1 tablespoon taco seasonings
1 tablespoon apple cider vinegar

1 tablespoon olive oil
900g chicken thighs, skinless, boneless

1. Rub the chicken thighs with taco seasonings and sprinkle with olive oil and apple cider vinegar. 2. Insert the crisper plate in the basket in zone 1, and transfer the chicken thighs to it. 3. Select AIR FRY mode, adjust the cooking temperature to 185°C and set the cooking time to 30 minutes. 4. Press the START/PAUSE button to begin cooking. 5. Flip the chicken thighs halfway through.
Per Serving: Calories 539; Fat 41.05g; Sodium 339mg; Carbs 1.85g; Fibre 0.3g; Sugar 0.25g; Protein 37.56g

Chicken Wings with Chopped Spinach

Prep time: 10 minutes | Cook time: 25 minutes | Serves: 4

30g fresh spinach, chopped
2 tablespoons olive oil

25g Parmesan, grated
455g chicken wings, skinless, boneless, chopped

1. Insert the crisper plate in the basket in zone 1, brush it with olive oil and then put the chicken thighs on it; top the chicken wings with chopped spinach and Parmesan cheese. 2. Select AIR FRY mode, adjust the cooking temperature to 190°C and set the cooking time to 25 minutes. 3. Press the START/PAUSE button to begin cooking. 4. Serve hot.
Per Serving: Calories 231; Fat 11.15g; Sodium 180mg; Carbs 3.11g; Fibre 0.2g; Sugar 0.14g; Protein 27.97g

Tasty Chicken Thighs

Prep time: 5 minutes | Cook time: 25 minutes | Serves: 4

4 chicken thighs, skinless, boneless
1 tablespoon coconut oil
1 teaspoon ground cumin

½ teaspoon salt
½ teaspoon smoked paprika

1. Mix the chicken thighs with coconut oil, cumin, salt, and smoked paprika. 2. Insert the crisper plate in the basket in zone 1, and transfer the chicken thighs to it. 3. Select AIR FRY mode, adjust the cooking temperature to 190°C and set the cooking time to 25 minutes. 4. Press the START/PAUSE button to begin cooking. 5. Serve hot.
Per Serving: Calories 459; Fat 35.61g; Sodium 448mg; Carbs 0.88g; Fibre 0.2g; Sugar 0.04g; Protein 32.02g

Keto TSO Chicken Breast

Prep time: 25 minutes | Cook time: 25 minutes | Serves: 4

455g chicken breast, skinless, boneless, chopped
1 tablespoon avocado oil
1 teaspoon ground black pepper
1 teaspoon salt
1 tablespoon coconut aminos
50g almond flour

1 teaspoon Erythritol
1 chili pepper, chopped
50g spring onions, chopped
1 teaspoon coconut oil
60ml of water

1. Rub the chicken with avocado oil, ground black pepper, salt, and coconut aminos. 2. Add water and marinate the chicken for 15 minutes. 3. Combine the almond flour, Erythritol, chili pepper, and spring onions in a bowl. 4. Coat the chicken in the almond flour mixture and transfer to the crisper plate in the basket. 5. Select AIR FRY mode, adjust the cooking temperature to 190°C and set the cooking time to 22 minutes. 6. Press the START/PAUSE button to begin cooking. 7. Flip the chicken breast halfway through cooking.
Per Serving: Calories 248; Fat 15.27g; Sodium 660mg; Carbs 2.74g; Fibre 0.8g; Sugar 1.01g; Protein 24.26g

Cream Chicken Breast

Prep time: 10 minutes | Cook time: 25 minutes | Serves: 5

675g chicken breast, skinless, boneless
1 teaspoon ground paprika
½ teaspoon ground turmeric
2 teaspoons cream cheese

25g spring onions, chopped
1 teaspoon avocado oil
½ teaspoon salt

1. Rub the chicken breast with ground paprika, turmeric, and salt. 2. Insert the crisper plates in the baskets. 3. Divide the chicken breast between the baskets in zone 1 and zone 2; spray them with avocado oil, and then sprinkle the spring onions and cream cheese over them. 4. Select AIR FRY mode, adjust the cooking temperature to 190°C and set the cooking time to 25 minutes. 5. Press the MATCH COOK button and copy the zone 1 settings to zone 2. 6. Press the START/PAUSE button to begin cooking.
Per Serving: Calories 252; Fat 14.14g; Sodium 328mg; Carbs 0.94g; Fibre 0.4g; Sugar 0.26g; Protein 28.71g

Kung Pao Chicken Breast

Prep time: 50 minutes | Cook time: 20 minutes | Serves: 4

675g chicken breast, halved
1 tablespoon lemon juice
2 tablespoons mirin
60ml milk
2 tablespoons soy sauce
1 tablespoon olive oil

1 teaspoon ginger, peeled and grated
2 garlic cloves, minced
½ teaspoon salt
½ teaspoon Szechuan pepper
½ teaspoon xanthan gum

1. In a large ceramic dish, place the chicken, lemon juice, mirin, milk, soy sauce, olive oil, ginger, and garlic. Let it marinate for 30 minutes in your refrigerator. 2. Insert the crisper plate in the basket in zone 1, and transfer the chicken breast halves to it. 3. Select AIR FRY mode, adjust the cooking temperature to 190°C and set the cooking time to 14 minutes. 4. Press the START/PAUSE button to begin cooking. 5. Flip the chicken breast and baste with the reserved marinade after 10 minutes of cooking time. 6. When cooked, season the meat with salt and pepper. Set aside. 7. Add the marinade to the preheated frying pan over medium heat; add in xanthan gum. Let it cook for 5 to 6 minutes until the sauce thickens. 8. Spoon the sauce over the reserved chicken and serve immediately.
Per Serving: Calories 361; Fat 21.08g; Sodium 526mg; Carbs 4.19g; Fibre 0.4g; Sugar 2.71g; Protein 36.75g

Chicken Drumsticks with Jalapeno Peppers

Prep time: 5 minutes | Cook time: 25 minutes | Serves: 4

900g chicken drumsticks
2 jalapeno peppers, minced
1 tablespoon avocado oil

1 teaspoon ground black pepper
½ teaspoon garlic powder

1. In the mixing bowl, mix chicken drumsticks with jalapeno peppers, avocado oil, ground black pepper, and garlic powder. 2. Insert the crisper plate in the basket in zone 1, and transfer the chicken drumsticks to it. 3. Select AIR FRY mode, adjust the cooking temperature to 190°C and set the cooking time to 25 minutes. 4. Press the START/PAUSE button to begin cooking. 5. When done, serve warm.
Per Serving: Calories 401; Fat 24.42g; Sodium 241mg; Carbs 1.46g; Fibre 0.4g; Sugar 0.3g; Protein 42.21g

Chicken Tortillas

Prep time: 15 minutes | Cook time: 10 minutes | Serves: 2

2 keto tortillas
225g chicken fillet, cooked, shredded
1 jalapeno pepper, sliced

75g Parmesan, grated
1 teaspoon dried dill

1. In the mixing bowl, mix shredded chicken with jalapeno pepper, Parmesan, and dried dill. 2. Spread the mixture over the tortillas and fold them. 3. Insert the crisper plate in the basket in zone 1, and transfer the chicken tortillas to it. 4. Select AIR FRY mode, adjust the cooking temperature to 200°C and set the cooking time to 10 minutes. 5. Press the START/PAUSE button to begin cooking. 6. Flip the food halfway through cooking. 7. Serve hot.
Per Serving: Calories 599; Fat 22g; Sodium 924mg; Carbs 42.19g; Fibre 1.6g; Sugar 2.5g; Protein 55.15g

Provolone Chicken Breasts

Prep time: 5 minutes | Cook time: 25 minutes | Serves: 6

1.3kg chicken breast, skinless, boneless
1 tablespoon coconut oil
125g provolone cheese, shredded

1 teaspoon dried oregano
1 teaspoon dried coriander

1. Rub the chicken breast with dried oregano and coriander. 2. Brush the chicken breast with coconut oil. 3. Insert the crisper plates in the baskets. Divide the chicken breast between the baskets in zone 1 and zone 2. 4. Select AIR FRY mode, adjust the cooking temperature to 195°C and set the cooking time to 24minutes. 5. Press the MATCH COOK button and copy the zone 1 settings to zone 2. 6. Press the START/PAUSE button to begin cooking. 7. Top the chicken breast with Provolone cheese after 20 minutes of cooking time. 8. Enjoy.
Per Serving: Calories 493; Fat 29.54g; Sodium 350mg; Carbs 0.62g; Fibre 0.1g; Sugar 0.14g; Protein 53.35g

Easy Turkey Bacon

Prep time: 10 minutes | Cook time: 8 minutes | Serves: 2

200g turkey bacon, sliced
1 teaspoon olive oil

½ teaspoon liquid stevia

1. Sprinkle the turkey bacon with olive oil and liquid stevia. 2. Insert the crisper plate in the basket in zone 1, and transfer the turkey bacon to it. 3. Select AIR FRY mode, adjust the cooking temperature to 190°C and set the cooking time to 8 minutes. 4. Press the START/PAUSE button to begin cooking. 5. Flip the turkey bacon halfway through cooking.
Per Serving: Calories 374; Fat 36.02g; Sodium 1662mg; Carbs 7.24g; Fibre 3g; Sugar 0.04g; Protein 12.14g

Chicken Legs with Brussels Sprouts

Prep time: 30 minutes | Cook time: 20 minutes | Serves: 2

2 chicken legs
½ teaspoon paprika
½ teaspoon salt

½ teaspoon black pepper
225g Brussels sprouts
1 teaspoon dill, fresh or dried

1. Season the chicken legs with paprika, salt, and pepper. 2. Insert the crisper plates in the baskets. 3. Place the chicken legs in zone 1 and add the Brussels sprouts and dill to zone 2. 4. Select AIR FRY mode, adjust the cooking temperature to 190°C and set the cooking time to 20 minutes. 5. Select zone 2, set the AIR FRY mode, and adjust the cooking temperature to 190°C and cooking time to 15 minutes. 6. Press the SMART FINISH button, and then press the START/PAUSE button to begin cooking. 7. Flip the chicken legs and toss the Brussels sprouts halfway through cooking. 8. Serve and enjoy.
Per Serving: Calories 371; Fat 11.63g; Sodium 865mg; Carbs 10.99g; Fibre 4.7g; Sugar 2.56g; Protein 54.79g

Manchego Turkey Meatballs

Prep time: 15 minutes | Cook time: 15 minutes | Serves: 4

455g turkey mince
225g pork mince
1 egg, well beaten
1 teaspoon dried basil
1 teaspoon dried rosemary

25g Manchego cheese, grated
2 tablespoons yellow onions, finely chopped
1 teaspoon fresh garlic, finely chopped
Sea salt and ground black pepper, to taste

1. In a mixing bowl, combine all the ingredients until everything is well incorporated. 2. Shape the mixture into 2.5 cm balls. 3. Insert the crisper plates in the baskets. Divide the meatballs between the baskets in zone 1 and zone 2. 4. Select AIR FRY mode, adjust the cooking temperature to 190°C and set the cooking time to 7 minutes. 5. Press the MATCH COOK button and copy the zone 1 settings to zone 2. 6. Press the START/PAUSE button to begin cooking. 7. Flip the meatballs halfway through cooking. 8. Serve the meatballs with your favorite pasta.
Per Serving: Calories 782; Fat 66.38g; Sodium 231mg; Carbs 3.01g; Fibre 0.4g; Sugar 0.96g; Protein 40.53g

Turkey with Hoisin Sauce

Prep time: 45 minutes | Cook time: 40 minutes | Serves: 4

900g turkey drumsticks
2 tablespoons balsamic vinegar
2 tablespoons dry white wine
1 tablespoon sesame oil
For the Hoisin Sauce
2 tablespoons hoisin sauce

1 sprig rosemary, chopped
Salt and ground black pepper, to your liking
2½ tablespoons butter, melted

1 tablespoon mustard

1. Add the turkey drumsticks to a mixing dish; add the vinegar, wine, sesame oil, and rosemary. Let them marinate for 3 hours. 2. Season the turkey drumsticks with salt and black pepper; spread the melted butter over the surface of drumsticks. 3. Insert the crisper plates in the baskets. Divide the turkey drumsticks between the baskets in zone 1 and zone 2. 4. Select ROAST mode, adjust the cooking temperature to 175°C and set the cooking time to 40 minutes. 5. Press the MATCH COOK button and copy the zone 1 settings to zone 2. 6. Press the START/PAUSE button to begin cooking. 7. Flip the turkey drumsticks a few times during working. 8. While the turkey drumsticks are roasting, prepare the Hoisin sauce by mixing the ingredients. 9. Drizzle the turkey with the sauce mixture after 35 minutes of cooking time. 10. Let the dish rest about 10 minutes before carving and serving.
Per Serving: Calories 619; Fat 33.32g; Sodium 2491mg; Carbs 10.89g; Fibre 0.7g; Sugar 4.01g; Protein 64.47g

Turkey Breasts with Basil

Prep time: 60 minutes | Cook time: 58 minutes | Serves: 4

2 tablespoons olive oil
900g turkey breasts, bone-in skin-on
Coarse sea salt and ground black pepper, to taste

1 teaspoon fresh basil leaves, chopped
2 tablespoons lemon zest, grated

1. Rub olive oil on all sides of the turkey breasts; sprinkle with salt, pepper, basil, and lemon zest. 2. Insert the crisper plates in the baskets and line them with parchment paper. 3. Divide the turkey breasts between the baskets in zone 1 and zone 2 with skin-side up. 4. Select AIR FRY mode, adjust the cooking temperature to 165°C and set the cooking time to 58 minutes. 5. Press the MATCH COOK button and copy the zone 1 settings to zone 2. 6. Press the START/PAUSE button to begin cooking. 7. Flip the turkey breasts after 30 minutes of cooking time. 8. You can serve the dish with lemon wedges.
Per Serving: Calories 422; Fat 22.71g; Sodium 135mg; Carbs 1.59g; Fibre 0.2g; Sugar 0.77g; Protein 49.9g

Chicken Breasts with Sauce

Prep time: 30 minutes | Cook time: 30 minutes | Serves: 4

2 chicken breasts cut into bite-sized chunks
35g almond flour
For the Sauce
60ml dry white wine
2 tablespoons coconut aminos

160g spring onions, chopped
1 celery, chopped

120ml of chicken stock

1. Toss the chicken chunks with the almond flour, covering well. 2. Insert the crisper plate in the basket in zone 1, and transfer the chicken chunks to it. 3. Select AIR FRY mode, adjust the cooking temperature to 185°C and set the cooking time to 27 minutes. 4. Press the START/PAUSE button to begin cooking. 5. Add the vegetables after 20 minutes of cooking time. 6. In a sauté pan, whisk the remaining ingredients over a moderate flame; then, turn the heat to medium-low and simmer for 2 to 3 minutes. 7. Serve the chicken with the warm sauce and enjoy!
Per Serving: Calories 182; Fat 6.07g; Sodium 567mg; Carbs 3.24g; Fibre 1.1g; Sugar 1.15g; Protein 27.55g

Buttermilk Chicken Tenders

Prep time: 80 minutes | Cook time: 15 minutes | Serves: 4

180ml of buttermilk
675g chicken tenders
60g coconut flour
2 tablespoons flaxseed meal
Salt, to your liking

½ teaspoon pink peppercorns, freshly cracked
1 teaspoon shallot powder
½ teaspoon cumin powder
1½ teaspoons smoked cayenne pepper
1 tablespoon sesame oil

1. Place the buttermilk and chicken tenders in the mixing dish; gently stir to coat and let it soak for 1 hour. 2. Mix the coconut flour with flaxseed meal and all seasonings. Coat the soaked chicken tenders with the coconut flour mixture; now, dip them into the buttermilk. 3. Finally, dredge them in the coconut flour mixture. 4. Brush the prepared chicken tenders with sesame oil. 5. Insert the crisper plate in the basket in zone 1, and transfer the chicken thighs to it. 6. Select AIR FRY mode, adjust the cooking temperature to 185°C and set the cooking time to 15 minutes. 7. Press the START/PAUSE button to begin cooking. 8. Flip the chicken tenders once or twice during cooking. 9. Serve and enjoy.
Per Serving: Calories 516; Fat 28.15g; Sodium 880mg; Carbs 35.55g; Fibre 2g; Sugar 3.17g; Protein 30.75g

Herbs de Provence Chicken

Prep time: 25 minutes | Cook time: 25 minutes | Serves: 4

4 medium-sized skin-on chicken drumsticks
1½ teaspoons herbs de Provence
Salt and pepper, to your liking
1 tablespoon rice vinegar
2 tablespoons olive oil

2 garlic cloves, crushed
50g crushed canned tomatoes
1 small-size leek, thinly sliced
2 slices smoked bacon, chopped

1. Sprinkle the chicken drumsticks with herbs de Provence, salt and pepper; then, drizzle them with rice vinegar and olive oil. 2. Insert the crisper plates in the baskets. 3. Divide the chicken drumsticks between the baskets in zone 1 and zone 2. 4. Select AIR FRY mode, adjust the cooking temperature to 180°C and set the cooking time to 25 minutes. 5. Press the MATCH COOK button and copy the zone 1 settings to zone 2. 6. Press the START/PAUSE button to begin cooking. 7. Stir in the remaining ingredients after 10 minutes of cooking time. 8. Serve warm.
Per Serving: Calories 357; Fat 24.14g; Sodium 345mg; Carbs 8g; Fibre 2.3g; Sugar 3.98g; Protein 26.4g

Turkey Breasts with Parsley

Prep time: 25 minutes | Cook time: 25 minutes | Serves: 2

½ tablespoon minced fresh parsley
1½ tablespoons Worcestershire sauce
Sea salt flakes and cracked black peppercorns, to savor
1½ tablespoons olive oil

⅓ turkey breasts, halved
1½ tablespoons rice vinegar
½ teaspoon marjoram

1. In a bowl, mix all ingredients together; make sure to coat turkey breast well. 2. Set them aside to marinate the turkey breast halves for at least 3 hours. 3. Insert the crisper plate in the basket in zone 1, and transfer the turkey breast halves to it. 4. Select ROAST mode, adjust the cooking temperature to 200°C and set the cooking time to 23 minutes. 5. Press the START/PAUSE button to begin cooking. 6. Flip the breast halves halfway through cooking.
Per Serving: Calories 689; Fat 36.39g; Sodium 424mg; Carbs 2.74g; Fibre 0.1g; Sugar 1.34g; Protein 81.82g

Turkey Sausage with Cauliflower

Prep time: 45 minutes | Cook time: 40 minutes | Serves: 4

455g turkey mince
1 teaspoon garlic pepper
1 teaspoon garlic powder
⅓ teaspoon dried oregano
½ teaspoon salt

55g onions, chopped
½ head cauliflower, broken into florets
⅓ teaspoon dried basil
½ teaspoon dried thyme, chopped

1. In a mixing bowl, thoroughly combine the turkey mince, garlic pepper, garlic powder, oregano, salt, and onion; stir well to combine. 2. Form the mixture into 4 sausages. 3. Cook the sausages in a frying pan over medium heat for 12 minutes or until they are no longer pink. 4. Insert the crisper plate in the basket in zone 1; arrange the cauliflower florets onto the crisper plate, sprinkle them with thyme and basil, and spray them with pan spray, and then top them with the cooked turkey sausages. 5. Select ROAST mode, adjust the cooking temperature to 190°C and set the cooking time to 28 minutes. 6. Press the START/PAUSE button to begin cooking. 7. Toss the food halfway through cooking. 8. Serve warm.
Per Serving: Calories 566; Fat 50.54g; Sodium 352mg; Carbs 4.26g; Fibre 1.1g; Sugar 1.63g; Protein 22.7g

Turkey Breast with Indian Mint Sauce

Prep time: 35 minutes | Cook time: 35 minutes | Serves: 4

675g turkey breast, quartered
½ teaspoon hot paprika
120ml dry sherry
1 teaspoon salt
For the Indian Mint Sauce
80g sour cream
1 ½ tablespoons fresh roughly chopped mint

⅓ teaspoon shallot powder
2 cloves garlic, peeled and halved
Freshly cracked pink or green peppercorns, to taste

240g plain yogurt

1. Rub the garlic halves evenly over the surface of the turkey breast. 2. Add the dry sherry, shallot powder, hot paprika, salt, and cracked peppercorns. Allow it to marinate in your refrigerator for at least 1½ hours. 3. Insert the crisper plates in the baskets. Divide the turkey breast between the baskets in zone 1 and zone 2. 4. Select ROAST mode, adjust the cooking temperature to 185°C and set the cooking time to 32 minutes. 5. Press the MATCH COOK button and copy the zone 1 settings to zone 2. 6. Press the START/PAUSE button to begin cooking. 7. Flip the turkey breast halfway through cooking. 8. Mix up all of the sauce ingredients in a bowl to make the sauce. 9. Serve the meat warm with the sauce.
Per Serving: Calories 483; Fat 22.54g; Sodium 768mg; Carbs 11.96g; Fibre 1.1g; Sugar 9.1g; Protein 55.34g

White Wine Marinated Turkey Wings

Prep time: 30 minutes | Cook time: 28 minutes | Serves: 4

1 teaspoon freshly cracked pink peppercorns
225g turkey wings, cut into smaller pieces
2 teaspoon garlic powder

80ml white wine
½ teaspoon garlic salt
½ tablespoon coriander, ground

1. Toss all of the above ingredients in a mixing dish. Let the turkey wings marinate at least 3 hours. 2. Insert the crisper plate in the basket in zone 1, and transfer the turkey wings to it. 3. Select AIR FRY mode, adjust the cooking temperature to 180°C and set the cooking time to 28 minutes. 4. Press the START/PAUSE button to begin cooking. 5. Serve warm.
Per Serving: Calories 346; Fat 20.99g; Sodium 96mg; Carbs 2.09g; Fibre 0.3g; Sugar 0.25g; Protein 35.01g

Chicken Sausages & Cauliflower Gratin

Prep time: 45 minutes | Cook time: 35 minutes | Serves: 4

225g chicken sausages, smoked
225g ham, sliced
150g cauliflower rice
2 garlic cloves, minced
200g spinach
120g Ricotta cheese

50g cheese, grated
4 eggs
120g yogurt
120ml milk
Salt and ground black pepper, to taste
1 teaspoon smoked paprika

1. Insert the crisper plate in the basket in zone 1, and transfer the sausages to it. 2. Select AIR FRY mode, adjust the cooking temperature to 190°C and set the cooking time to 10 minutes. 3. Press the START/PAUSE button to begin cooking. 4. When cooked, set aside. 5. In a preheated saucepan, cook the cauliflower and garlic for 4 minutes, stirring frequently; remove from the heat, add the spinach and cover with the lid. 6. Allow the spinach to wilt completely. 7. In a mixing dish, thoroughly combine the cheese, eggs, yogurt, milk, salt, pepper, and paprika. 8. Transfer the sautéed mixture to the basket in zone 2; add the reserved sausage and ham, and then pour the cheese mixture over the food. 9. Select AIR FRY mode, adjust the cooking temperature to 190°C and set the cooking time to 30 minutes. 10. Serve warm.
Per Serving: Calories 427; Fat 27.05g; Sodium 1624mg; Carbs 13.95g; Fibre 2.5g; Sugar 4.92g; Protein 32.97g

Cajun Turkey Thighs

Prep time: 35 minutes | Cook time: 30 minutes | Serves: 4

900g turkey thighs, skinless and boneless
1 red onion, sliced
2 peppers, deveined and sliced
1 habanero pepper, deveined and minced

1 carrot, sliced
1 tablespoon Cajun seasoning mix
1 tablespoon fish sauce
480ml chicken stock

1. Transfer the turkey thighs to the basket in zone 1, add the onion, pepper and carrot, and sprinkle them with Cajun seasoning, and then add the fish sauce and chicken stock. 2. Select AIR FRY mode, adjust the cooking temperature to 180°C and set the cooking time to 30 minutes. 3. Press the START/PAUSE button to begin cooking. 4. Serve warm.

Per Serving: Calories 499; Fat 19.35g; Sodium 3824mg; Carbs 10.43g; Fibre 1.3g; Sugar 5.49g; Protein 66.65g

Chicken Drumsticks with Asparagus

Prep time: 30 minutes | Cook time: 30 minutes | Serves: 6

6 chicken drumsticks
675g asparagus ends trimmed
Marinade
3 tablespoons rapeseed oil
3 tablespoons soy sauce
3 tablespoons lime juice

3 heaping tablespoons shallots, minced
1 heaping teaspoon fresh garlic, minced
1 (2.5cm) piece fresh ginger, peeled and minced
1 teaspoon cajun seasoning
Coarse sea salt and ground black pepper, to taste

1. In a ceramic bowl, mix all ingredients for the marinade. Add the chicken drumsticks and let them marinate at least 5 hours in the refrigerator. 2. Drain the chicken drumsticks and discard the marinade. 3. Insert the crisper plates in the baskets. Divide the chicken drumsticks between the baskets in zone 1 and zone 2. 4. Select AIR FRY mode, adjust the cooking temperature to 190°C and set the cooking time to 22 minutes. 5. Press the MATCH COOK button and copy the zone 1 settings to zone 2. 6. Press the START/PAUSE button to begin cooking. 7. Flip the chicken drumsticks halfway through cooking. 8. Add the reserved marinade to the preheated frying pan , add the asparagus and cook them for 5 minutes. 9. Serve the meat with the asparagus.

Per Serving: Calories 435; Fat 19.79g; Sodium 413mg; Carbs 8.6g; Fibre 2.9g; Sugar 4.25g; Protein 54.09g

Mediterranean Duck Breasts

Prep time: 25 minutes | Cook time: 25 minutes | Serves: 4

675g smoked duck breasts, boneless
1 tablespoon yellow mustard
2 tablespoons ketchup, low-carb
8 pearl onions peeled

125g chicken stock
2 egg yolks, whisked
1 teaspoon rosemary, finely chopped

1. Insert the crisper plate in the basket in zone 1, and transfer the smoked duck breasts to it. 2. Select AIR FRY mode, adjust the cooking temperature to 185°C and set the cooking time to 22 minutes. 3. Press the START/PAUSE button to begin cooking. 4. Smear the mustard and ketchup on the meat and top the meat with pearl onions after 15 minutes of cooking time. 5. When cooked, the skin of the duck breast should be crispy and golden brown. 6. Slice the duck breasts and reserve. Drain off the duck fat from the basket. 7. Add the reserved 1 tablespoon of duck fat to the pan and warm it over medium heat; add chicken stock and bring to a boil. 8. Gently fold in the whisked egg yolks and rosemary. Reduce the heat to low and cook until the gravy has thickened slightly. Spoon the warm gravy over the reserved duck breasts. Enjoy!

Per Serving: Calories 625; Fat 22.34g; Sodium 275mg; Carbs 50.65g; Fibre 6.1g; Sugar 33.42g; Protein 55.68g

Turkey Breast with Celery

Prep time: 50 minutes | Cook time: 45 minutes | Serves: 6

1.1kg turkey breasts
1 tablespoon fresh rosemary, chopped
1 teaspoon sea salt

½ teaspoon ground black pepper
1 onion, chopped
1 celery stalk, chopped

1. Insert the crisper plates in the baskets. Divide the turkey breasts between the baskets in zone 1 and zone 2, and add the rosemary, salt, and black pepper. 2. Select AIR FRY mode, adjust the cooking temperature to 180°C and set the cooking time to 45 minutes. 3. Press the MATCH COOK button and copy the zone 1 settings to zone 2. 4. Press the START/PAUSE button to begin cooking. 5. Add the onion and celery after 30 minutes of cooking time. 6. Serve warm.
Per Serving: Calories 306; Fat 13.32g; Sodium 502mg; Carbs 2.21g; Fibre 0.5g; Sugar 1.01g; Protein 41.68g

Parmesan Chicken Tenders

Prep time: 20 minutes | Cook time: 12 minutes | Serves: 6

1 lime
900g chicken tenderloins cut up
100g Parmesan cheese, grated
1 tablespoon olive oil
Sea salt and ground black pepper, to taste

1 teaspoon cayenne pepper
⅓ teaspoon ground cumin
1 teaspoon chili powder
1 egg

1. Squeeze the lime juice all over the chicken. 2. In a mixing bowl, thoroughly combine the Parmesan, olive oil, salt, black pepper, cayenne pepper, cumin, and chili powder. 3. In another shallow bowl, whisk the egg until well beaten. Dip the chicken tenderloins in the egg, then in parmesan mixture. 4. Insert the crisper plates in the baskets. Divide the chicken tenderloins between the baskets in zone 1 and zone 2. 5. Select AIR FRY mode, adjust the cooking temperature to 190°C and set the cooking time to 12 minutes. 6. Press the MATCH COOK button and copy the zone 1 settings to zone 2. 7. Press the START/PAUSE button to begin cooking. 8. Flip the meat halfway through cooking. 9. Serve immediately.
Per Serving: Calories 291; Fat 12.86g; Sodium 299mg; Carbs 2.98g; Fibre 0.4g; Sugar 0.61g; Protein 39.06g

Mexican Mole

Prep time: 35 minutes | Cook time: 35 minutes | Serves: 4

8 chicken thighs, skinless, bone-in
1 tablespoon peanut oil
Sea salt and ground black pepper, to taste
Mole sauce:
1 tablespoon peanut oil
1 onion, chopped
1 ounce dried negro chilies, stemmed, seeded, and chopped

2 garlic cloves, peeled and halved
1 large-sized fresh tomatoes, pureed
35g chocolate, chopped
1 teaspoon dried Mexican oregano
½ teaspoon ground cumin
1 teaspoon coriander seeds
A pinch of ground cloves
30g almonds, slivered and toasted

1. Toss the chicken thighs with the peanut oil, salt, and black pepper. 2. Insert the crisper plate in the basket in zone 1, and transfer the chicken thighs to it. 3. Select AIR FRY mode, adjust the cooking temperature to 190°C and set the cooking time to 22 minutes. 4. Press the START/PAUSE button to begin cooking. 5. Flip the chicken thighs after 12 minutes of cooking time. 6. Heat 1 tablespoon of peanut oil in a saucepan over medium-high heat; sauté the onion, chilies and garlic for 2 minutes or until fragrant. 7. Stir in the tomatoes, chocolate, oregano, cumin, coriander seeds, and cloves. Let it simmer until the sauce has slightly thickened. 8. Add the reserved chicken thighs to the basket in zone 2, and add the sauce. 9. Select AIR FRY mode, adjust the cooking temperature to 180°C and set the cooking time to 10 minutes. 10. Press the START/PAUSE button to begin cooking. 11. Garnish the dish with slivered almonds.
Per Serving: Calories 967; Fat 72.43g; Sodium 558mg; Carbs 12.46g; Fibre 4.3g; Sugar 3.51g; Protein 66.19g

Spicy Turkey Meatloaf

Prep time: 55 minutes | Cook time: 55 minutes | Serves: 6

900g turkey breasts, ground
225g Cheddar cheese, cubed
120ml turkey stock
⅓ teaspoon hot paprika
3 eggs, lightly beaten
1 ½ tablespoon olive oil
2 cloves garlic, pressed

1½ teaspoons dried rosemary
80g yellow onion, chopped
40g ground almonds
½ teaspoon black pepper
A few dashes of Tabasco sauce
1 teaspoon seasoned salt
120g tomato sauce

1. Heat the olive oil in a medium-sized saucepan that is placed over a moderate flame; sauté the onions, garlic, and dried rosemary for 3 to 4 minutes until just tender. 2. Combine all the ingredients, minus the tomato sauce, in a mixing dish together with the sautéed mixture. 3. Shape the mixture into meatloaf and top with the tomato sauce. 4. Transfer the meatloaf to the basket in zone 1. 5. Select ROAST mode, adjust the cooking temperature to 195°C and set the cooking time to 47 minutes. 6. Press the START/PAUSE button to begin cooking. 7. Serve warm.
Per Serving: Calories 447; Fat 23.23g; Sodium 1420mg; Carbs 10.78g; Fibre 1.6g; Sugar 6.18g; Protein 45.37g

Ranch Chicken Wings

Prep time: 25 minutes | Cook time: 22 minutes | Serves: 3

25g almond meal
25g flaxseed meal
2 tablespoons butter, melted
6 tablespoons parmesan cheese, preferably freshly grated

1 tablespoon Ranch seasoning mix
2 tablespoons oyster sauce
6 chicken wings, bone-in

1. In a re-sealable bag, place the almond meal, flaxseed meal, butter, parmesan, Ranch seasoning mix, and oyster sauce. Add the chicken wings and shake to coat on all sides. 2. Insert the crisper plate in the basket in zone 1, and transfer the chicken wings to it. 3. Select AIR FRY mode, adjust the cooking temperature to 190°C and set the cooking time to 22 minutes. 4. Press the START/PAUSE button to begin cooking. 5. Flip the chicken wings halfway through cooking. 6. You can serve warm with your favorite dipping sauce.
Per Serving: Calories 274; Fat 18.5g; Sodium 827mg; Carbs 8.43g; Fibre 4.3g; Sugar 0.54g; Protein 18.54g

Chicken Legs & Cauliflower

Prep time: 30 minutes | Cook time: 30 minutes | Serves: 4

900g chicken legs
2 tablespoons olive oil
1 teaspoon sea salt
½ teaspoon ground black pepper
1 teaspoon smoked paprika
1 teaspoon dried marjoram

1 (455g) head cauliflower, broken into small florets
2 garlic cloves, minced
35g Pecorino Romano cheese, freshly grated
½ teaspoon dried thyme
Salt, to taste

1. Toss the chicken legs with the olive oil, salt, black pepper, paprika, and marjoram. 2. Insert the crisper plate in the basket in zone 1, and transfer the chicken legs to it. 3. Select AIR FRY mode, adjust the cooking temperature to 190°C and set the cooking time to 16 minutes. 4. Press the START/PAUSE button to begin cooking. 5. Flip the chicken legs halfway through cooking. 6. Toss the cauliflower florets with garlic, cheese, thyme, and salt. 7. When the cooking time is up, add the cauliflower florets, and resume cooking the food at 205°Cfor 12 minutes more. 8. Serve warm.
Per Serving: Calories 390; Fat 18.91g; Sodium 1008mg; Carbs 5.89g; Fibre 1.7g; Sugar 1.64g; Protein 47.39g

Chapter 4 Beef, Pork, and Lamb

Lamb Burgers

Prep time: 15 minutes | Cook time: 16 minutes | Serves: 2

250g. lamb fillet, minced
25g broccoli, shredded
1 tablespoon dried coriander

½ teaspoon onion powder
1 teaspoon coconut oil, melted

1. Mix minced lamb fillet with broccoli, dried coriander, and onion powder. 2. Form the mixture into burgers and sprinkle them with coconut oil. 3. Insert the crisper plate in the basket in zone 1, and transfer the burgers to it. 4. Select AIR FRY mode, adjust the cooking temperature to 180°C and set the cooking time to 16 minutes. 5. Press the START/PAUSE button to begin cooking. 6. Flip the burgers halfway through cooking. 7. Serve warm.
Per Serving: Calories 386; Fat 26.13g; Sodium 110mg; Carbs 0.64g; Fibre 0.2g; Sugar 0.06g; Protein 34.99g

Curry Tender Bites

Prep time: 25 minutes | Cook time: 30 minutes | Serves: 4

455g lamb fillet, cubed
1 teaspoon curry paste

60g coconut cream
1 teaspoon olive oil

1. Mix all ingredients in the mixing bowl and leave for 20 minutes to marinate. 2. Insert the crisper plate in the basket in zone 1, and transfer the lamb fillet to it. 3. Select AIR FRY mode, adjust the cooking temperature to 185°C and set the cooking time to 30 minutes. 4. Press the START/PAUSE button to begin cooking. 5. Serve warm.
Per Serving: Calories 351; Fat 25.47g; Sodium 87mg; Carbs 1.28g; Fibre 0.6g; Sugar 0.01g; Protein 28.42g

Coriander Lamb Sausages

Prep time: 25 minutes | Cook time: 20 minutes | Serves: 4

4 sausage links
900g lamb mince
1 tablespoon dried coriander

1 teaspoon salt
1 tablespoon avocado oil

1. Mix lamb mince with dried coriander and salt. 2. Fill the sausage links with lamb mixture and brush with avocado oil. 3. Insert the crisper plate in the basket in zone 1, and transfer the sausage links to it. 4. Select AIR FRY mode, adjust the cooking temperature to 200°Cand set the cooking time to 20 minutes. 5. Press the START/PAUSE button to begin cooking. 6. Flip the food halfway through cooking.
Per Serving: Calories 533; Fat 36.19g; Sodium 933mg; Carbs 2.47g; Fibre 0.7g; Sugar 0g; Protein 50.75g

Lamb Loin with Caraway Seeds

Prep time: 10 minutes | Cook time: 30 minutes | Serves: 4

900g lamb loin
120ml apple cider vinegar
1 tablespoon coconut oil, melted

1 tablespoon caraway seeds
½ teaspoon salt

1. Marinate the lamb loin in the mixture of apple cider vinegar, coconut oil, caraway seeds, and salt. 2. Insert the crisper plate in the basket in zone 1, and transfer the lamb loin to it. 3. Select AIR FRY mode, adjust the cooking temperature to 190°C and set the cooking time to 30 minutes. 4. Press the START/PAUSE button to begin cooking. 5. Serve warm.
Per Serving: Calories 371; Fat 19.29g; Sodium 467mg; Carbs 4.34g; Fibre 0.7g; Sugar 2.99g; Protein 45.68g

Butter Rack of Lamb

Prep time: 10 minutes | Cook time: 50 minutes | Serves: 4

400g rack of lamb, chopped
115g butter, softened

1 tablespoon dried parsley
1 teaspoon salt

1. Sprinkle the rack of lamb with dried parsley and salt. 2. Insert the crisper plate in the basket in zone 1, and transfer the meat to it. 3. Select AIR FRY mode, adjust the cooking temperature to 180°C and set the cooking time to 50 minutes. 4. Press the START/PAUSE button to begin cooking. 5. Serve warm.
Per Serving: Calories 385; Fat 32.79g; Sodium 840mg; Carbs 0.08g; Fibre 0g; Sugar 0.03g; Protein 23.69g

Lamb Cutlets

Prep time: 10 minutes | Cook time: 16 minutes | Serves: 4

900g lamb cutlets
1 teaspoon minced ginger

1 tablespoon avocado oil
½ teaspoon ground black pepper

1. Mix minced ginger with avocado oil and ground black pepper. 2. Mix lamb cutlets with the ginger mixture. 3. Insert the crisper plate in the basket in zone 1, and transfer the lamb cutlets to it. 4. Select AIR FRY mode, adjust the cooking temperature to 190°C and set the cooking time to 16 minutes. 5. Press the START/PAUSE button to begin cooking. 6. Flip the lamb cutlets halfway through cooking.
Per Serving: Calories 614; Fat 41.66g; Sodium 173mg; Carbs 0.62g; Fibre 0.1g; Sugar 0.3g; Protein 55.73g

Lamb Leg

Prep time: 2 hours | Cook time: 35 minutes | Serves: 2

300g leg of lamb, boneless
1 teaspoon dried thyme
½ teaspoon dried coriander

1 teaspoon onion powder
1 tablespoon coconut aminos
1 tablespoon avocado oil

1. Mix all ingredients from the list above in the mixing bowl and leave to marinate for 2 hours. 2. Insert the crisper plate in the basket in zone 1, and transfer the food to it. 3. Select AIR FRY mode, adjust the cooking temperature to 190°C and set the cooking time to 35 minutes. 4. Press the START/PAUSE button to begin cooking. 5. Stir the meat from time to time during cooking. 6. Serve warm.
Per Serving: Calories 296; Fat 16.02g; Sodium 119mg; Carbs 1.33g; Fibre 0.3g; Sugar 0.28g; Protein 34.58g

Almond Meatballs

Prep time: 15 minutes | Cook time: 30 minutes | Serves: 4

675g lamb, ground
25g almonds, grinded
1 tablespoon coconut shred

1 teaspoon dried dill
1 tablespoon olive oil

1. Mix lamb mince with almonds, coconut shred, and dried dill. 2. Make the mixture into meatballs. 3. Insert the crisper plate in the basket in zone 1, and transfer the chicken thighs to it. 4. Spray the meatballs with olive oil. 5. Select AIR FRY mode, adjust the cooking temperature to 175°C and set the cooking time to 30 minutes. 6. Press the START/PAUSE button to begin cooking. 7. Serve warm.
Per Serving: Calories 509; Fat 35.61g; Sodium 133mg; Carbs 1.96g; Fibre 1g; Sugar 0.41g; Protein 43.32g

Rib Eye Steaks

Prep time: 15 minutes | Cook time: 18 minutes | Serves: 4

455g beef rib eye steak, bone-in (4 steaks)
1 tablespoon coconut oil
1 teaspoon onion powder
½ teaspoon lemon zest, grated

½ teaspoon ground black pepper
1 teaspoon chipotle powder
1 teaspoon salt

1. In the shallow bowl, mix coconut oil with onion powder, lemon zest, ground black pepper, chipotle powder, and salt. 2. Rub the beef rib-eye steak with the chipotle mixture. 3. Insert the crisper plate in the basket in zone 1, and transfer the steaks to it. 4. Select AIR FRY mode, adjust the cooking temperature to 195°C and set the cooking time to 18 minutes. 5. Press the START/PAUSE button to begin cooking. 6. Flip the steaks halfway through cooking. 7. Serve warm.
Per Serving: Calories 331; Fat 27.19g; Sodium 647mg; Carbs 1.52g; Fibre 0.3g; Sugar 0.38g; Protein 20.56g

Spiced Lamb Cutlets

Prep time: 15 minutes | Cook time: 50 minutes | Serves: 4

525g lamb cutlets
1 teaspoon white pepper
4 tablespoons avocado oil
1 teaspoon dried basil

1 tablespoon garlic powder
1 tablespoon ground coriander
1 tablespoon lemon zest, grated
3 tablespoons apple cider vinegar

1. Chop the lamb cutlets roughly. 2. Coat the lamb cutlets with the remaining ingredients. 3. Insert the crisper plate in the basket in zone 1, and transfer the lamb cutlets to it. 4. Select AIR FRY mode, adjust the cooking temperature to 185°C and set the cooking time to 20 minutes. 5. Press the START/PAUSE button to begin cooking. 6. Serve warm.
Per Serving: Calories 514; Fat 39.08g; Sodium 115mg; Carbs 2.64g; Fibre 0.5g; Sugar 0.21g; Protein 37.02g

Beef Goulash

Prep time: 70 minutes | Cook time: 65 minutes | Serves: 4

Sea salt and cracked black pepper, to taste
1 teaspoon Hungarian paprika
675g beef chuck roast, boneless, cut into bite-sized cubes
2 teaspoons sunflower oil
1 medium-sized leek, chopped
2 garlic cloves, minced

2 bay leaves
1 teaspoon caraway seeds.
480ml roasted vegetable stock
1 ripe tomato, pureed
2 tablespoons red wine
2 peppers, chopped
1 celery stalk, peeled and diced

1. Add the salt, black pepper, Hungarian paprika, and beef to a re-sealable bag; shake the bag to coat well. 2. Heat the oil in a frying pan over medium-high flame; sauté the leeks, garlic, bay leaves, and caraway seeds for about 4 minutes or until fragrant. 3. Transfer them to a lightly greased baking pan. 4. Brown the beef in the frying pan by stirring occasionally and then add to the baking pan. 5. Add the vegetable stock, tomato, and red wine. 6. Transfer the baking pan to the basket in zone 1. 7. Select BAKE mode, adjust the cooking temperature to 160°C and set the cooking time to 60 minutes. 8. Press the START/PAUSE button to begin cooking. 9. Add the peppers and celery after 40 minutes of cooking time. 10. Serve warm.
Per Serving: Calories 416; Fat 18.04g; Sodium 432mg; Carbs 16.34g; Fibre 3.3g; Sugar 5.36g; Protein 49.11g

Peppermint Lamb Chops

Prep time: 10 minutes | Cook time: 15 minutes | Serves: 4

455g lamb chops
1 teaspoon peppermint

1 teaspoon avocado oil
2 tablespoons lemon juice

1. Sprinkle the lamb chops with peppermint, avocado oil, and lemon juice. 2. Insert the crisper plate in the basket in zone 1, and transfer the lamb chops to it. 3. Select AIR FRY mode, adjust the cooking temperature to 205°C and set the cooking time to 12 minutes. 4. Press the START/PAUSE button to begin cooking. 5. Flip the lamb chops halfway through cooking. 6. Serve warm.
Per Serving: Calories 363; Fat 31.34g; Sodium 64mg; Carbs 0.54g; Fibre 0g; Sugar 0.19g; Protein 18.54g

Clove Lamb Cutlets

Prep time: 10 minutes | Cook time: 30 minutes | Serves: 4

8 lamb cutlets
1 teaspoon ground clove

1 teaspoon salt
Cooking spray

1. Sprinkle the lamb cutlets with ground clove and salt. 2. Insert the crisper plate in the basket in zone 1, and transfer the lamb cutlets to it. 3. Select AIR FRY mode, adjust the cooking temperature to 180°C and set the cooking time to 30 minutes. 4. Press the START/PAUSE button to begin cooking. 5. Flip the lamb cutlets halfway through cooking. 6. Serve warm.
Per Serving: Calories 460; Fat 14.13g; Sodium 964mg; Carbs 0.34g; Fibre 0.2g; Sugar 0.01g; Protein 78.05g

Simple Lamb Chops

Prep time: 10 minutes | Cook time: 20 minutes | Serves: 4

4 lamb chops
4 garlic cloves, minced

1 teaspoon saffron
Cooking spray

1. Sprinkle the lamb chops with garlic cloves and saffron. 2. Spray the lamb chops with cooking spray. 3. Insert the crisper plate in the basket in zone 1, and transfer the lamb chops to it. 4. Select AIR FRY mode, adjust the cooking temperature to 180°C and set the cooking time to 20 minutes. 5. Press the START/PAUSE button to begin cooking. 6. Flip the lamb chops halfway through cooking.
Per Serving: Calories 168; Fat 7.94g; Sodium 89mg; Carbs 1.11g; Fibre 0.1g; Sugar 0.03g; Protein 23.19g

Marjoram Lamb Chops

Prep time: 10 minutes | Cook time: 25 minutes | Serves: 4

900g lamb chops
1 teaspoon dried marjoram
1 teaspoon salt

1 tablespoon coconut cream
1 teaspoon coconut oil, melted

1. In the shallow bowl, mix dried marjoram, salt, coconut cream, and coconut oil. 2. Carefully rub the lamb chops with marjoram mixture. 3. Insert the crisper plate in the basket in zone 1, and transfer the lamb chops to it. 4. Select AIR FRY mode, adjust the cooking temperature to 190°C and set the cooking time to 25 minutes. 5. Press the START/PAUSE button to begin cooking. 6. Serve warm.
Per Serving: Calories 726; Fat 62.83g; Sodium 709mg; Carbs 0.34g; Fibre 0.1g; Sugar 0.01g; Protein 37.17g

Chopped Beef Oxtails

Prep time: 5 minutes | Cook time: 65 minutes | Serves: 5

900g beef oxtail, roughly chopped
1 teaspoon salt
240ml of water
1 teaspoon keto tomato paste

1 teaspoon ground black pepper
1 teaspoon Erythritol
1 teaspoon avocado oil

1. Mix up all of the ingredients and then transfer them to the basket in zone 1. 2. Select ROAST mode, adjust the cooking temperature to 180°C and set the cooking time to 65 minutes. 3. Press the START/PAUSE button to begin cooking. 4. Serve warm.
Per Serving: Calories 252; Fat 11.28g; Sodium 623mg; Carbs 0.58g; Fibre 0.2g; Sugar 0.14g; Protein 37.34g

Lamb Sauce

Prep time: 5 minutes | Cook time: 30 minutes | Serves: 4

455g lamb, minced
120g heavy cream

50g Parmesan, grated
1 teaspoon coconut oil

1. Mix minced lamb with heavy cream and coconut oil. 2. Insert the crisper plate in the basket in zone 1, and transfer the meat to it. 3. Select AIR FRY mode, adjust the cooking temperature to 185°C and set the cooking time to 20 minutes. 4. Press the START/PAUSE button to begin cooking. 5. Mix in the Parmesan and cook the food at 190°C for 10 minutes more.
Per Serving: Calories 404; Fat 26.46g; Sodium 255mg; Carbs 6.09g; Fibre 0g; Sugar 0.63g; Protein 33.78g

Lamb Chops with Yogurt

Prep time: 20 minutes | Cook time: 30 minutes | Serves: 4

900g lamb chops
240g Plain yogurt
1 teaspoon dried thyme

1 teaspoon salt
1 teaspoon olive oil

1. In the mixing bowl, mix Plain yogurt, dried thyme, salt, and olive oil. 2. Put the lamb chops in the yogurt mixture and leave for 10 minutes to marinate. 3. Insert the crisper plate in the basket in zone 1, and transfer the lamb chops to it. 4. Select AIR FRY mode, adjust the cooking temperature to 190°C and set the cooking time to 30 minutes. 5. Press the START/PAUSE button to begin cooking. 6. Serve warm.
Per Serving: Calories 751; Fat 63.52g; Sodium 737mg; Carbs 2.9g; Fibre 0g; Sugar 2.85g; Protein 39.15g

Lamb Balls

Prep time: 15 minutes | Cook time: 15 minutes | Serves: 4

455g minced lamb
1 teaspoon flax meal
½ teaspoon chili powder

1 egg, beaten
Cooking spray

1. Mix minced lamb with flax meal, chili powder, and egg. 2. Make the balls from the lamb mixture. 3. Spray the balls with cooking spray. 4. Insert the crisper plate in the basket in zone 1, and transfer the meatballs to it. 5. Select AIR FRY mode, adjust the cooking temperature to 200°C and set the cooking time to 15 minutes. 6. Press the START/PAUSE button to begin cooking. 7. Serve warm.
Per Serving: Calories 379; Fat 24.93g; Sodium 183mg; Carbs 0.73g; Fibre 0.1g; Sugar 0.25g; Protein 35.51g

Tuscan Beef Chops

Prep time: 20 minutes | Cook time: 15 minutes | Serves: 3

3 sprigs fresh thyme, chopped
80ml herb vinegar
2 teaspoons Tuscan seasoning

3 beef chops
2 teaspoons garlic powder
Salt and ground black pepper, to taste

1. Toss the beef chops with the other ingredients. 2. Insert the crisper plate in the basket in zone 1, and transfer the beef chops to it. 3. Select AIR FRY mode, adjust the cooking temperature to 200°C and set the cooking time to 16 minutes. 4. Press the START/PAUSE button to begin cooking. 5. Flip the beef chops once or twice during cooking. 6. Serve warm.
Per Serving: Calories 198; Fat 15.18g; Sodium 179mg; Carbs 4.46g; Fibre 0.8g; Sugar 1.13g; Protein 10.1g

Sirloin Steak with Mushroom Sauce

Prep time: 20 minutes | Cook time: 15 minutes | Serves: 5

2 tablespoons butter
900g sirloin, cut into four pieces
Salt and cracked black pepper, to taste
1 teaspoon cayenne pepper
½ teaspoon dried rosemary
½ teaspoon dried dill

¼ teaspoon dried thyme
455g Cremini mushrooms, sliced
240g sour cream
1 teaspoon mustard
½ teaspoon curry powder

1. Add the sirloin, salt, black pepper, cayenne pepper, rosemary, dill, and thyme to the basket in zone 1. 2. Select ROAST mode, adjust the cooking temperature to 200°C and set the cooking time to 15 minutes. 3. Press the START/PAUSE button to begin cooking. 4. Stir in the mushrooms, sour cream, mustard, and curry powder after 10 minutes of cooking time. 5. Serve warm.
Per Serving: Calories 330; Fat 14.68g; Sodium 270mg; Carbs 7.64g; Fibre 1.4g; Sugar 2.59g; Protein 41.4g

Blade Steak with Green Beans

Prep time: 25 minutes | Cook time: 15 minutes | Serves: 4

2 garlic cloves, smashed
2 teaspoons sunflower oil
½ teaspoon cayenne pepper
1 tablespoon Cajun seasoning

675g blade steak
200g green beans
½ teaspoon Tabasco pepper sauce
Sea salt and ground black pepper, to taste

1. Mix the garlic, oil, cayenne pepper, and Cajun seasoning to make a paste. Rub it over both sides of the blade steak. 2. Insert the crisper plate in the basket in zone 1, and transfer the chicken thighs to it. 3. Select AIR FRY mode, adjust the cooking temperature to 165°C and set the cooking time to 21 minutes. 4. Press the START/PAUSE button to begin cooking. 5. Flip the steak after 13 minutes of cooking time. 6. Heat the green beans in a saucepan. Add a few tablespoons of water, Tabasco, salt, and black pepper; heat them for 10 minutes or until the green beans wilt. 7. Serve the roasted blade steak with green beans on the side.
Per Serving: Calories 505; Fat 32.77g; Sodium 260mg; Carbs 6.24g; Fibre 2g; Sugar 1.44g; Protein 43.95g

Beef with feta Cheese

Prep time: 25 minutes | Cook time: 21 minutes | Serves: 3

50g feta cheese, cut into sticks
2 teaspoons paprika
2 teaspoons dried thyme
70g shallots, peeled and chopped
3 beef tenderloins, cut in half lengthwise
2 teaspoons dried basil

80ml homemade bone stock
2 tablespoon olive oil
3 cloves garlic, minced
360g tomato puree, no sugar added
1 teaspoon ground black pepper, or more to taste
1 teaspoon fine sea salt, or more to taste

1. Season the beef tenderloin with the salt, ground black pepper, and paprika; place a piece of the feta cheese in the middle. 2. Tie each tenderloin with a kitchen string; drizzle them with olive oil and reserve. 3. Stir the garlic, shallots, bone stock, and tomato puree in the basket. 4. Select ROAST mode, adjust the cooking temperature to 190°C and set the cooking time to 21 minutes. 5. Press the START/PAUSE button to begin cooking. 6. Add the reserved beef along with basil and thyme after 7 minutes of cooking time. 7. Serve warm.
Per Serving: Calories 463; Fat 25.07g; Sodium 1255mg; Carbs 18.15g; Fibre 4g; Sugar 8.81g; Protein 42.1g

Cubed Beef with Garlic–Mayo Sauce

Prep time: 1 hour 22 minutes | Cook time: 20 minutes | Serves: 4

675g beef, cubed
120g full fat sour cream
120ml white wine
2 teaspoons dried rosemary
1½ tablespoon herb vinegar
1 teaspoon sweet paprika

3 cloves garlic, minced
2 tablespoons extra-virgin olive oil
2 teaspoons dried basil
1 tablespoon mayonnaise
Salt and ground black pepper, to taste

1. In a large-sized mixing bowl, whisk together the oil, wine, and beef. Now, stir in the seasonings and herb vinegar. Cover the bowl and marinate the meat for at least 50 minutes. 2. Transfer the mixture to the basket in zone 1. 3. Select ROAST mode, adjust the cooking temperature to 190°C and set the cooking time to 18 minutes. 4. Press the START/PAUSE button to begin cooking. 5. Toss the food halfway through cooking. 6. Mix the sour cream with the mayonnaise and garlic to make the sauce. 7. Serve the dish with sauce.
Per Serving: Calories 300; Fat 14.05g; Sodium 280mg; Carbs 7.33g; Fibre 0.6g; Sugar 1.15g; Protein 36.73g

Pork Spareribs & Peppers

Prep time: 55 minutes | Cook time: 35 minutes | Serves: 4

455g pork spareribs individually cut
1 teaspoon seasoned salt
½ teaspoon ground black pepper
1 tablespoon sweet paprika

½ teaspoon mustard powder
2 tablespoons sesame oil
4 peppers, seeded

1. Toss and rub the spices all over the pork ribs; drizzle them with 1 tablespoon of sesame oil. 2. Toss the peppers with the remaining 1 tablespoon of oil. 3. Insert the crisper plates in the baskets. 4. Place the pork ribs in zone 1 and add the peppers to zone 2. 5. Select AIR FRY mode, adjust the cooking temperature to 180°C and set the cooking time to 15 minutes. 6. Select zone 2, set the ROAST mode, and adjust the cooking temperature to 200°C and cooking time to 15 minutes. 7. Press the SMART FINISH button, and then press the START/PAUSE button to begin cooking. 8. Serve the warm spareribs with the roasted peppers on the side.
Per Serving: Calories 325; Fat 23.91g; Sodium 658mg; Carbs 5.74g; Fibre 1.4g; Sugar 2.76g; Protein 21.94g

Bacon–Pork Pops

Prep time: 30 minutes | Cook time: 30 minutes | Serves: 6

240ml cream of celery soup
1 (340ml) can coconut milk, unsweetened
2 tablespoons tamari sauce
1 teaspoon yellow mustard
Salt and freshly ground white pepper, to taste
½ teaspoon cayenne pepper

½ teaspoon chili powder
1 teaspoon curry powder
900g pork tenderloin, cut into bite-sized cubes
100g bacon, cut into pieces
12 bamboo skewers, soaked in water

1. In a large pot, bring the cream of the celery soup, coconut milk, tamari sauce, mustard, salt, white pepper, cayenne pepper, chili powder, and curry powder to a boil. 2. Reduce the heat to simmer; cook them for 13 minutes until the sauce is heated through, about 13 minutes. 3. Add the pork, gently stir, and let them stay in the refrigerator for 2 hours. 4. Thread the pork onto the skewers, alternating the cubes of meat with the pieces of bacon. 5. Insert the crisper plates in the baskets. Divide the skewers between the baskets in zone 1 and zone 2. 6. Select ROAST mode, adjust the cooking temperature to 190°C and set the cooking time to 15 minutes. 7. Press the MATCH COOK button and copy the zone 1 settings to zone 2. 8. Press the START/PAUSE button to begin cooking. 9. Flip the skewers a few times during cooking. 10. Serve warm.
Per Serving: Calories 308; Fat 12.12g; Sodium 597mg; Carbs 6.28g; Fibre 1.9g; Sugar 2.05g; Protein 42.62g

Burgers with Blue Cheese

Prep time: 20 minutes | Cook time: 45 minutes | Serves: 6

225g blue cheese, sliced
2 teaspoons dried basil
1 teaspoon smoked paprika
900g pork mince
2 tablespoons tomato puree

2 small-sized onions, peeled and chopped
½ teaspoon ground black pepper
3 garlic cloves, minced
1 teaspoon fine sea salt

1. In a mixing dish, combine the pork, onion, garlic, tomato puree, and seasonings; mix to combine well. 2. Form the pork mixture into six patties. 3. Insert the crisper plates in the baskets. Divide the patties between the baskets in zone 1 and zone 2. 4. Select AIR FRY mode, adjust the cooking temperature to 195°C and set the cooking time to 41 minutes. 5. Press the MATCH COOK button and copy the zone 1 settings to zone 2. 6. Press the START/PAUSE button to begin cooking. 7. Flip the patties and adjust the temperature to 185°C after 23 minutes of cooking time. 8. Place the prepared burgers on a serving platter; top with blue cheese and serve warm.
Per Serving: Calories 545; Fat 37.98g; Sodium 759mg; Carbs 4.34g; Fibre 0.8g; Sugar 1.6g; Protein 44.28g

Pork & Pepper Meatloaf

Prep time: 35 minutes | Cook time: 25 minutes | Serves: 4

455g pork, ground
50g Parmesan cheese, grated
1 ½ tablespoons green garlic, minced
1½ tablespoon fresh coriander, minced
½ tablespoon fish sauce
⅓ teaspoon dried basil

1 leek, chopped
1 Serrano pepper, chopped
2 tablespoons tomato puree
½ teaspoons dried thyme
Salt and ground black pepper, to taste

1. Combine all ingredients in a large-sized mixing dish. Form the mixture into a meatloaf. 2. Transfer the meatloaf to the basket in zone 1. 3. Select BAKE mode, adjust the cooking temperature to 185°C and set the cooking time to 23 minutes. 4. Press the START/PAUSE button to begin cooking. 5. Allow the meatloaf to rest for 10 minutes before slicing and serving.
Per Serving: Calories 317; Fat 16.16g; Sodium 473mg; Carbs 7.96g; Fibre 0.9g; Sugar 2g; Protein 33.65g

Pork Chops with Coriander

Prep time: 25 minutes | Cook time: 18 minutes | Serves: 6

35g parmesan, grated
Roughly chopped fresh coriander, to taste
2 teaspoons Cajun seasonings
Nonstick cooking spray
2 eggs, beaten

3 tablespoons almond meal
1 teaspoon seasoned salt
Garlic & onion spice blend, to taste
6 pork chops
⅓ teaspoon freshly cracked black pepper

1. Coat the pork chops with Cajun seasonings, salt, pepper, and the spice blend on all sides. 2. Add the almond meal to a plate. 3. In a shallow dish, whisk the egg until pale and smooth. 4. Place the parmesan in the third bowl. 5. Dredge each pork piece in the almond meal; then, coat them with the egg; finally, coat them with the parmesan. Spritz them with cooking spray on both sides. 6. Insert the crisper plates in the baskets. Divide the pork rinds between the baskets in zone 1 and zone 2. 7. Select AIR FRY mode, adjust the cooking temperature to 175°C and set the cooking time to 18 minutes. 8. Press the MATCH COOK button and copy the zone 1 settings to zone 2. 9. Press the START/PAUSE button to begin cooking. 10. Make sure to taste for doneness after first 12 minutes of cooking. 11. Garnish the dish with fresh coriander.
Per Serving: Calories 410; Fat 21.52g; Sodium 591mg; Carbs 1.27g; Fibre 0.2g; Sugar 0.47g; Protein 49.24g

Tangy Pork Chops

Prep time: 35 minutes | Cook time: 15 minutes | Serves: 5

5 pork chops
80ml vermouth
½ teaspoon paprika
2 sprigs thyme, only leaves, crushed
½ teaspoon dried oregano
Fresh parsley, to serve

1 teaspoon garlic salt
½ lemon, cut into wedges
1 teaspoon freshly cracked black pepper
3 tablespoons lemon juice
3 cloves garlic, minced
2 tablespoons rapeseed oil

1. Heat the rapeseed oil in a sauté pan over a moderate heat; sweat the garlic until just fragrant. 2. Remove the pan from the heat and pour in the lemon juice and vermouth. Throw in the seasonings. Dump the sauce into a baking dish, along with the pork chops. 3. Tuck the lemon wedges among the pork chops. 4. Insert the crisper plate in the basket in zone 1, and transfer the food to it. 5. Select AIR FRY mode, adjust the cooking temperature to 175°C and set the cooking time to 27 minutes. 6. Press the START/PAUSE button to begin cooking. 7. Serve warm.
Per Serving: Calories 412; Fat 23.07g; Sodium 89mg; Carbs 4.52g; Fibre 0.4g; Sugar 1.62g; Protein 40.56g

Ham Egg Cups

Prep time: 20 minutes | Cook time: 12 minutes | Serves: 2

2 eggs
¼ teaspoon dried or fresh marjoram
2 teaspoons chili powder
⅓ teaspoon salt

30g steamed kale
¼ teaspoon dried or fresh rosemary
4 pork ham slices
⅓ teaspoon ground black pepper, or more to taste

1. Divide the kale and ham among 2 ramekins; crack an egg into each ramekin. Sprinkle them with seasonings. 2. Transfer the ramekins to the basket in zone 1. 3. Select BAKE mode, adjust the cooking temperature to 170°C and set the cooking time to 15 minutes. 4. Press the START/PAUSE button to begin cooking. 5. Serve warm with spicy tomato ketchup and pickles.
Per Serving: Calories 1226; Fat 40.03g; Sodium 6938mg; Carbs 8.91g; Fibre 1.2g; Sugar 6.74g; Protein 208.62g

Pork mince Omelet

Prep time: 20 minutes | Cook time: 15 minutes | Serves: 2

4 garlic cloves, peeled and minced
½ tablespoon fresh basil, chopped
150g pork mince
⅓ teaspoon ground black pepper
½ small-sized onion, peeled and finely chopped

1 ½ tablespoons olive oil
3 medium-sized eggs, beaten
½ jalapeno pepper, seeded and chopped
4 tablespoons cream cheese
⅓ teaspoon salt

1.In a nonstick frying pan that is preheated over a moderate flame, heat the oil; then, sweat the onion, garlic and pork mince in the hot oil. 2. Spritz a suitable baking dish with a cooking spray. 3. Add the sautéed mixture and the remaining ingredients to the baking dish. 4. Transfer the baking dish to the basket in zone 1. 5. Select BAKE mode, adjust the cooking temperature to 160°C and set the cooking time to 15 minutes. 6. Press the START/PAUSE button to begin cooking. 7. Serve the dish with the salad of your choice.
Per Serving: Calories 515; Fat 40.63g; Sodium 669mg; Carbs 6.09g; Fibre 0.6g; Sugar 2.62g; Protein 30.42g

Pork Belly with Aromatics

Prep time: 1 hour 15 minutes | Cook time: 70 minutes | Serves: 4

455g pork belly
2 garlic cloves, halved
1 teaspoon shallot powder
1 teaspoon sea salt
1 teaspoon dried basil

1 teaspoon dried oregano
1 teaspoon dried thyme
1 teaspoon dried marjoram
1 teaspoon ground black pepper
1 lime, juiced

1. Blanch the pork belly in a pot of boiling water for 10 to 13 minutes. 2. Pat it dry with a kitchen towel. Poke holes all over the skin. 3. Mix the remaining ingredients to make the rub. Massage the rub all over the pork belly. Drizzle lime juice all over the meat; place the pork belly in the refrigerator for 3 hours. 4. Insert the crisper plate in the basket in zone 1, and transfer the chicken thighs to it. 5. Select AIR FRY mode, adjust the cooking temperature to 160°C and set the cooking time to 55 minutes. 6. Press the START/PAUSE button to begin cooking. 7. Adjust the cooking temperature to 180°C after 35 minutes of cooking time. 8. Serve warm.
Per Serving: Calories 146; Fat 6.17g; Sodium 1859mg; Carbs 3.95g; Fibre 0.5g; Sugar 1.86g; Protein 19.67g

Pork Stuffed Peppers

Prep time: 30 minutes | Cook time: 25 minutes | Serves: 3

3 peppers, stems and seeds removed
1 tablespoon rapeseed oil
80g onions, chopped
1 teaspoon fresh garlic, minced
1 Mexican chili pepper, finely chopped
455g lean pork, minced

½ teaspoon sea salt
½ teaspoon black pepper
1 tablespoon Mexican oregano
1 ripe tomato, pureed
75g cheese, grated

1. Cook the peppers in boiling salted water for 4 minutes. 2. In a nonstick frying pan , heat the rapeseed oil over medium heat. Then, sauté the onions, garlic and Mexican chili pepper until tender and fragrant. 3. Stir in the pork mince and continue sautéing until the pork has browned; drain off the excess fat. 4. Stir in the salt, black pepper, Mexican oregano, and pureed tomato. 5. Divide the filling among the peppers. 6. Insert the crisper plate in the basket in zone 1, and transfer the stuffed peppers to it. 7. Select BAKE mode, adjust the cooking temperature to 190°Cand set the cooking time to 19 minutes. 8. Press the START/PAUSE button to begin cooking. 9. Top the peppers with grated feta cheese after 13 minutes of cooking time. 10. Serve warm.
Per Serving: Calories 350; Fat 19.09g; Sodium 2558mg; Carbs 14.73g; Fibre 2.1g; Sugar 9.21g; Protein 32.39g

Twisted Pork Chops

Prep time: 20 minutes | Cook time: 15 minutes | Serves: 3

60ml balsamic vinegar
3 centre-cut loin pork chops
25g almond meal
2 tablespoons golden flaxseed meal
1 teaspoon turmeric powder
1 egg

1 teaspoon mustard
Salt , to taste
¼ teaspoon freshly ground black pepper
50g parmesan, grated
½ teaspoon garlic powder
1 teaspoon shallot powder

1. Drizzle the balsamic vinegar over pork chops and spread to evenly coat. 2. Place the almond meal, flaxseed meal, and turmeric in a shallow bowl. In another bowl, whisk the eggs, mustard, salt, and black pepper. 3. In the third bowl, mix the pork rinds with the garlic powder and shallot powder. 4. Dredge the pork chops in the almond meal mixture, then in the egg, followed by the parmesan mixture. 5. Insert the crisper plate in the basket in zone 1, and transfer the pork chops to it. 6. Select AIR FRY mode, adjust the cooking temperature to 200°C and set the cooking time to 14 minutes. 7. Press the START/PAUSE button to begin cooking. 8. Flip the pork chops and spray them with cooking oil halfway through cooking. 9. Serve warm.
Per Serving: Calories 583; Fat 28.3g; Sodium 326mg; Carbs 7.33g; Fibre 2.3g; Sugar 3.61g; Protein 69.94g

Chinese Pork Shoulder

Prep time: 25 minutes | Cook time: 15 minutes | Serves: 3

2 tablespoons coconut aminos
2 tablespoons Shaoxing wine
2 garlic cloves, minced
1 teaspoon fresh ginger, minced

1 tablespoon coriander stems and leaves, finely chopped
455g boneless pork shoulder
2 tablespoons sesame oil

1. In a large-sized ceramic dish, thoroughly combine the coconut aminos, Shaoxing wine, garlic, ginger, and coriander; add the pork shoulder and allow it to marinate for 2 hours in the refrigerator. 2. Insert the crisper plate in the basket in zone 1, and transfer the pork shoulder to it, reserve the marinade. 3. Select AIR FRY mode, adjust the cooking temperature to 200°C and set the cooking time to 17 minutes. 4. Press the START/PAUSE button to begin cooking. 5. Flip the meat and baste with the marinade halfway through cooking. 6. Cook the remaining marinade in a preheated frying pan over medium heat until thickened. 7. Brush the pork shoulder with the sauce and enjoy!
Per Serving: Calories 269; Fat 17.24g; Sodium 1714mg; Carbs 3.42g; Fibre 0.2g; Sugar 2.55g; Protein 26.06g

Minced Lamb Sticks

Prep time: 15 minutes | Cook time: 30 minutes | Serves: 4

1 teaspoon minced garlic
25g chives, chopped

1 teaspoon dried dill
900g lamb, minced

1. Mix lamb mince with dried dill, chives, and minced garlic. 2. Make the sticks from the lamb mixture. 3. Insert the crisper plate in the basket in zone 1, and transfer the sticks to it. 4. Select AIR FRY mode, adjust the cooking temperature to 180°C and set the cooking time to 30 minutes. 5. Press the START/PAUSE button to begin cooking. 6. Serve warm.
Per Serving: Calories 585; Fat 38.28g; Sodium 173mg; Carbs 0.83g; Fibre 0.3g; Sugar 0.14g; Protein 55.97g

Mini Meatloaves

Prep time: 50 minutes | Cook time: 50 minutes | Serves: 4

455g pork mince
225g beef mince
1 package onion soup mix
50g Romano cheese, grated
2 eggs
1 pepper, chopped
1 Serrano pepper, minced

2 spring onions, chopped
2 cloves garlic, finely chopped
Sea salt and black pepper, to your liking
120g tomato paste
1 tablespoon brown mustard
1 teaspoon smoked paprika

1. In a large mixing bowl, thoroughly combine all ingredients for meatloaves. 2. Shape the mixture into four mini loaves. 3. Mix all ingredients for the glaze. 4. Insert the crisper plate in the basket in zone 1, and transfer the meat loaves to it. 5. Select AIR FRY mode, adjust the cooking temperature to 195°C and set the cooking time to 49 minutes. 6. Press the START/PAUSE button to begin cooking. 7. Spread the glaze over the mini meatloaves after 43 minutes of cooking time. 8. Serve warm.
Per Serving: Calories 707; Fat 45.62g; Sodium 843mg; Carbs 13.18g; Fibre 2.5g; Sugar 6.16g; Protein 59.49g

Pork & Carrots

Prep time: 1 hour 15 minutes | Cook time: 55 minutes | Serves: 4

1 tablespoon peanut oil
675g pork loin, cut into 4 pieces
Coarse sea salt and ground black pepper, to taste
½ teaspoon onion powder
1 teaspoon garlic powder
½ teaspoon cayenne pepper

½ teaspoon dried rosemary
½ teaspoon dried basil
½ teaspoon dried oregano
455g celery, cut into matchsticks
1 tablespoon coconut oil, melted

1. Drizzle 1 tablespoon of peanut oil all over the pork loin. Season the meat with salt, black pepper, onion powder, garlic powder, cayenne pepper, rosemary, basil, and oregano. 2. Toss the carrots with melted coconut oil. 3. Insert the crisper plates in the baskets. 4. Place the meat in zone 1 and add the carrots to zone 2. 5. Select AIR FRY mode, adjust the cooking temperature to 180°C and set the cooking time to 55 minutes. 6. Select zone 2, set the AIR FRY mode, and adjust the cooking temperature to 190°C and cooking time to 15 minutes. 7. Press the SMART FINISH button, and then press the START/PAUSE button to begin cooking. 8. Flip the pork every 15 minutes during cooking. 9. Serve the warm pork loin with the carrots on the side.
Per Serving: Calories 442; Fat 25.87g; Sodium 186mg; Carbs 5.52g; Fibre 2.3g; Sugar 2.16g; Protein 44.79g

Chapter 5 Fish and Seafood

Garlic Cod Fillets

Prep time: 15 minutes | Cook time: 15 minutes | Serves: 4

4 cod fillets
¼ teaspoon fine sea salt
¼ teaspoon ground black pepper, or more to taste
1 teaspoon cayenne pepper
120ml non-dairy milk

20g fresh Italian parsley, coarsely chopped
1 teaspoon dried basil
½ teaspoon dried oregano
1 Italian pepper, chopped
4 garlic cloves, minced

Coat the inside of a baking dish with a thin layer of vegetable oil.
1. Season the cod fillets with salt, pepper, and cayenne pepper. 2. Puree the remaining ingredients in your food processor. Toss the fish fillets with this mixture. 3. Insert the crisper plate in the basket in zone 1, and transfer the fish fillets to it. 4. Select AIR FRY mode, adjust the cooking temperature to 190°C and set the cooking time to 12 minutes. 5. Press the START/PAUSE button to begin cooking. 6. Serve warm.
Per Serving: Calories 502; Fat 42.74g; Sodium 568mg; Carbs 10.87g; Fibre 5.9g; Sugar 1.55g; Protein 20.35g

Halibut Steaks with Vermouth

Prep time: 15 minutes | Cook time: 10 minutes | Serves: 4

455g halibut steaks
Salt and pepper, to your liking
1 teaspoon dried basil
2 tablespoons honey
60ml vegetable oil

2 ½ tablespoons Worcester sauce
1 tablespoon freshly squeezed lemon juice
2 tablespoons vermouth
1 tablespoon fresh parsley leaves, coarsely chopped

1. Place all the ingredients in a large-sized mixing dish. Gently stir to coat the fish evenly. 2. Insert the crisper plate in the basket in zone 1, and transfer the halibut steaks to it. 3. Select ROAST mode, adjust the cooking temperature to 200°C and set the cooking time to 10 minutes. 4. Press the START/PAUSE button to begin cooking. 5. Flip the fish steaks halfway through cooking. 6. Serve warm.
Per Serving: Calories 382; Fat 29.4g; Sodium 215mg; Carbs 11.94g; Fibre 0.6g; Sugar 10.55g; Protein 16.76g

Parmesan Fish Fillets

Prep time: 15 minutes | Cook time: 15 minutes | Serves: 4

100g parmesan, grated
1 teaspoon garlic powder
½ teaspoon shallot powder
1 egg, well whisked

4 white fish fillets
Salt and ground black pepper, to taste
Fresh Italian parsley, to serve

1. Place the parmesan cheese in a shallow bowl. 2. In another bowl, combine the garlic powder, shallot powder, and the beaten egg. 3. Generously season the fish fillets with salt and pepper. Dip each fillet into the beaten egg. 4. Roll the fillets over the parmesan mixture. 5. Insert the crisper plate in the basket in zone 1, and transfer the fillets to it. 6. Select AIR FRY mode, adjust the cooking temperature to 190°C and set the cooking time to 12 minutes. 7. Press the START/PAUSE button to begin cooking. 8. Garnish the dish with fresh parsley and enjoy.
Per Serving: Calories 260; Fat 7.13g; Sodium 320mg; Carbs 9.92g; Fibre 0.2g; Sugar 1.07g; Protein 37.25g

Sardines Frittas

Prep time: 1 hour 15 minutes | Cook time: 10 minutes | Serves: 4

675g sardines, cleaned and rinsed
Salt and ground black pepper, to savor
1 tablespoon Italian seasoning mix

1 tablespoon lemon juice
1 tablespoon soy sauce
2 tablespoons olive oil

1. Pat the sardines dry with a kitchen towel. Add salt, black pepper, Italian seasoning mix, lemon juice, soy sauce, and olive oil; marinate them for 30 minutes. 2. Insert the crisper plate in the basket in zone 1, and transfer the sardines to it. 3. Select AIR FRY mode, adjust the cooking temperature to 175°C and set the cooking time to 13 minutes. 4. Press the START/PAUSE button to begin cooking. 5. Increase the cooking temperature to 195°C after 5 minutes of cooking time. 6. Place the sardines in a nice serving platter and enjoy.
Per Serving: Calories 437; Fat 26.98g; Sodium 738mg; Carbs 3.57g; Fibre 0.5g; Sugar 1.67g; Protein 42.5g

Delicious Tuna Casserole

Prep time: 20 minutes | Cook time: 20 minutes | Serves: 4

5 eggs, beaten
½ chili pepper, deveined and finely minced
1 ½ tablespoons sour cream
⅓ teaspoon dried oregano
½ tablespoon sesame oil

60g yellow onions, chopped
230g canned tuna
½ pepper, deveined and chopped
⅓ teaspoon dried basil
Fine sea salt and ground black pepper, to taste

1. Heat the sesame oil in a nonstick frying pan over a moderate flame; sweat the onions and peppers for 4 minutes or until they are just fragrant. 2. Add chopped canned tuna and stir until heated through. 3. Transfer all of them to the basket in zone 1. 4. Bake the food at 160°C for 12 minutes. 5. Garnish the dish with Tabasco sauce before enjoying.
Per Serving: Calories 273; Fat 15.84g; Sodium 338mg; Carbs 4.36g; Fibre 0.5g; Sugar 2.29g; Protein 27.94g

Curried Medium Halibut Fillets

Prep time: 20 minutes | Cook time: 15 minutes | Serves: 4

2 medium-sized halibut fillets
1 teaspoon curry powder
½ teaspoon ground coriander
Salt and freshly cracked mixed peppercorns, to taste
1 ½ tablespoons olive oil

50g Parmesan cheese, grated
2 eggs
½ teaspoon hot paprika
A few drizzles of Tabasco sauce

1. In a bowl, combine the parmesan cheese with olive oil. 2. In another shallow bowl, thoroughly whisk the egg. 3. Evenly drizzle the halibut fillets with Tabasco sauce; add hot paprika, curry, coriander, salt, and cracked mixed peppercorns. 4. Dip each fish fillet into the whisked egg; now, roll each of them over the parmesan mix. 5. Insert the crisper plates in the baskets. Divide the fish fillets between the baskets in zone 1 and zone 2. 6. Select AIR FRY mode, adjust the cooking temperature to 185°C and set the cooking time to 10 minutes. 7. Press the MATCH COOK button and copy the zone 1 settings to zone 2. 8. Press the START/PAUSE button to begin cooking. 9. Serve the dish over creamed salad if desired.
Per Serving: Calories 288; Fat 21.13g; Sodium 485mg; Carbs 6.51g; Fibre 3g; Sugar 0.72g; Protein 17.93g

Herbed Prawns

Prep time: 40 minutes | Cook time: 5 minutes | Serves: 4

½ tablespoon fresh basil leaves, chopped
675g prawns, shelled and deveined
1 ½ tablespoons olive oil
3 cloves garlic, minced

1 teaspoon smoked cayenne pepper
½ teaspoon fresh mint, roughly chopped
½ teaspoon ginger, freshly grated
1 teaspoon sea salt

1. In a mixing dish, combine all of the ingredients; toss them until everything is well combined and let it stand for about 28 minutes. 2. Insert the crisper plate in the basket in zone 1, and transfer the food to it. 3. Select AIR FRY mode, adjust the cooking temperature to 200°C and set the cooking time to 4 minutes. 4. Press the START/PAUSE button to begin cooking. 5. Serve and enjoy.

Per Serving: Calories 261; Fat 9.65g; Sodium 2073mg; Carbs 1.05g; Fibre 0.2g; Sugar 0.07g; Protein 39.96g

Salmon Fish Cakes

Prep time: 2 hours 15 minutes | Cook time: 15 minutes | Serves: 4

½ teaspoon chipotle powder
½ teaspoon butter, at room temperature
⅓ teaspoon smoked cayenne pepper
½ teaspoon dried parsley flakes
⅓ teaspoon ground black pepper
455g salmon, chopped into 1 cm pieces

1½ tablespoons milk
½ white onion, peeled and finely chopped
1 teaspoon fine sea salt
2 tablespoons coconut flour
2 tablespoons parmesan cheese, grated

1. Place all ingredients in a large-sized mixing dish. 2. Shape the mixture into cakes and roll each cake over seasoned breadcrumbs. After that, refrigerate the meat cakes for about 2 hours. 3. Insert the crisper plate in the basket in zone 1, and transfer the fish cakes to it. 4. Select AIR FRY mode, adjust the cooking temperature to 200°C and set the cooking time to 13 minutes. 5. Press the START/PAUSE button to begin cooking. 6. Serve the dish warm with a dollop of sour cream if desired.

Per Serving: Calories 208; Fat 9.58g; Sodium 1135mg; Carbs 4.47g; Fibre 0.6g; Sugar 2.76g; Protein 24.77g

Mediterranean Scallops

Prep time: 2 hours 12 minutes | Cook time: 15 minutes | Serves: 2

1½ tablespoons coconut aminos
1 tablespoon Mediterranean seasoning mix
60g shallots, chopped
½ tablespoon balsamic vinegar
1½ tablespoons olive oil

1 clove garlic, chopped
½ teaspoon ginger, grated
455g scallops, cleaned
Chicory, for garnish

1. In a small-sized sauté pan over a moderate flame, simmer all ingredients, minus scallops and Belgian endive. Allow this mixture to cool down completely. 2. Add the scallops and let them marinate for at least 2 hours in the refrigerator. 3. Insert the crisper plate in the basket in zone 1, and transfer the scallops to it and spray the with oil. 4. Select AIR FRY mode, adjust the cooking temperature to 175°Cand set the cooking time to 10 minutes. 5. Press the START/PAUSE button to begin cooking. 6. Flip the scallops halfway through cooking. 7. Serve immediately with Chicory.

Per Serving: Calories 277; Fat 11.31g; Sodium 1213mg; Carbs 13.33g; Fibre 1.1g; Sugar 2.3g; Protein 28.05g

Tuna with Red Onions

Prep time: 20 minutes | Cook time: 15 minutes | Serves: 4

4 tuna steaks
225g red onions
4 teaspoons olive oil
1 teaspoon dried rosemary
1 teaspoon dried marjoram

1 tablespoon cayenne pepper
½ teaspoon sea salt
½ teaspoon black pepper, preferably freshly cracked
1 lemon, sliced

1. Insert the crisper plates in the baskets in zone 1 and zone 2, and transfer the tuna steaks to them, and then top them with pearl onions, sprinkle olive oil, rosemary, marjoram, cayenne pepper, salt, and black pepper over them. 2. Select BAKE mode, adjust the cooking temperature to 205°C and set the cooking time to 10 minutes. 3. Press the MATCH COOK button and copy the zone 1 settings to zone 2. 4. Press the START/PAUSE button to begin cooking. 5. Serve warm with lemon slices.
Per Serving: Calories 318; Fat 5.96g; Sodium 396mg; Carbs 7.24g; Fibre 1.5g; Sugar 2.85g; Protein 56.23g

Fried Haddock Fillets

Prep time: 20 minutes | Cook time: 15 minutes | Serves: 2

2 haddock fillets
50g Parmesan cheese, freshly grated
1 teaspoon dried parsley flakes
1 egg, beaten

½ teaspoon coarse sea salt
¼ teaspoon ground black pepper
¼ teaspoon cayenne pepper
2 tablespoons olive oil

1. Pat dry the haddock fillets and set aside. 2. In a shallow bowl, thoroughly combine the parmesan and parsley flakes. 3. In a separate shallow bowl, whisk the egg with salt, black pepper, and cayenne pepper. 4. Dip the haddock fillets into the egg. Then, dip the fillets into the parmesan mixture until well coated on all sides. 5. Drizzle the olive oil all over the fish fillets. 6. Insert the crisper plate in the basket in zone 1, and transfer the cod fillets to it. 7. Select AIR FRY mode, adjust the cooking temperature to 180°C and set the cooking time to 13 minutes. 8. Press the START/PAUSE button to begin cooking. 9. Serve hot.
Per Serving: Calories 435; Fat 26.21g; Sodium 1496mg; Carbs 4.7g; Fibre 0.2g; Sugar 0.66g; Protein 43.25g

Prawns Skewers

Prep time: 15 minutes | Cook time: 5 minutes | Serves: 4

675g prawns
60ml vermouth
2 cloves garlic, crushed
Salt, to taste

¼ teaspoon black pepper, freshly ground
2 tablespoons olive oil
8 skewers, soaked in water for 30 minutes
1 lemon, cut into wedges

1. Add the prawns, vermouth, garlic, salt, black pepper, and olive oil in a ceramic bowl; let it sit for 1 hour in your the refrigerator. 2. Discard the marinade and toss the prawns with flour. Thread the prawns on to skewers and transfer to the lightly greased cooking basket. 3. Insert the crisper plates in the baskets. Divide the skewers between the baskets in zone 1 and zone 2. 4. Select AIR FRY mode, adjust the cooking temperature to 205°C and set the cooking time to 5 minutes. 5. Press the MATCH COOK button and copy the zone 1 settings to zone 2. 6. Press the START/PAUSE button to begin cooking. 7. Flip the skewers halfway through cooking. 8. Serve warm.
Per Serving: Calories 259; Fat 9.11g; Sodium 1521mg; Carbs 3.46g; Fibre 0.1g; Sugar 1.47g; Protein 34.92g

Lobster Tails with Olives

Prep time: 20 minutes | Cook time: 7 minutes | Serves: 5

900g fresh lobster tails, cleaned and halved, in shells
2 tablespoons butter, melted
1 teaspoon onion powder
1 teaspoon cayenne pepper

Salt and ground black pepper, to taste
2 garlic cloves, minced
180g green olives

1. In a plastic closeable bag, thoroughly combine all ingredients; shake to combine well. 2. Insert the crisper plates in the baskets. 3. Divide the coated lobster tails between the baskets in zone 1 and zone 2. 4. Select AIR FRY mode, adjust the cooking temperature to 200°C and set the cooking time to 7 minutes. 5. Press the MATCH COOK button and copy the zone 1 settings to zone 2. 6. Press the START/PAUSE button to begin cooking. 7. Flip the lobster tails halfway through cooking. 8. Serve the dish with green olives and enjoy!
Per Serving: Calories 189; Fat 6.14g; Sodium 814mg; Carbs 1.86g; Fibre 0.3g; Sugar 0.55g; Protein 30.38g

King Prawns

Prep time: 10 minutes | Cook time: 8 minutes | Serves: 2

12 king prawns, rinsed
1 tablespoon coconut oil
½ teaspoon piri piri powder
Salt and ground black pepper, to taste

1 teaspoon garlic paste
1 teaspoon onion powder
½ teaspoon cumin powder
1 teaspoon curry powder

1. In a mixing bowl, toss all ingredients until the prawns are well coated on all sides. 2. Insert the crisper plate in the basket in zone 1, and transfer the prawns to it. 3. Select AIR FRY mode, adjust the cooking temperature to 180°C and set the cooking time to 8 minutes. 4. Press the START/PAUSE button to begin cooking. 5. Flip the prawns halfway through cooking. 6. Serve over hot rice if desired.
Per Serving: Calories 272; Fat 8.28g; Sodium 274mg; Carbs 4.34g; Fibre 1.1g; Sugar 1.28g; Protein 46.49g

Tuna Patties

Prep time: 2 hours 20 minutes | Cook time: 20 minutes | Serves: 4

455g canned tuna, drained
1 egg, whisked
1 garlic clove, minced
2 tablespoons shallots, minced
100g Romano cheese, grated
Sea salt and ground black pepper, to taste

1 tablespoon sesame oil
Cheese Sauce
1 tablespoon butter
240ml beer
2 tablespoons cheddar cheese, grated

1. In a mixing bowl, thoroughly combine the tuna, egg, garlic, shallots, Romano cheese, salt, and black pepper. 2. Shape the tuna mixture into four patties and place in your refrigerator for 2 hours. 3. Brush the patties with sesame oil on both sides. 4. Insert the crisper plate in the basket in zone 1, and transfer the tuna patties to it. 5. Select AIR FRY mode, adjust the cooking temperature to 180°C and set the cooking time to 14 minutes. 6. Press the START/PAUSE button to begin cooking. 7. Melt the butter in a pan over a moderate heat. Add the beer and whisk until it starts bubbling. 8. Stir in the grated cheese and cook for 3 to 4 minutes longer or until the cheese has melted. 9. Spoon the sauce over the fish patties and serve immediately.
Per Serving: Calories 457; Fat 30.85g; Sodium 834mg; Carbs 7.13g; Fibre 0.5g; Sugar 2.38g; Protein 37.99g

Snapper Fillets

Prep time: 30 minutes | Cook time: 30 minutes | Serves: 2

120ml full-fat coconut milk
2 tablespoons lemon juice
1 teaspoon fresh ginger, grated

2 snapper fillets
1 tablespoon olive oil
Salt and white pepper, to taste

1. Place the milk, lemon juice, and ginger in a glass bowl; add fish and let it marinate for 1 hour. 2. Insert the crisper plate in the basket in zone 1, and transfer the fish to it and spray the food with oil. 3. Select AIR FRY mode, adjust the cooking temperature to 200°C and set the cooking time to 15 minutes. 4. Press the START/ PAUSE button to begin cooking. 5. Flip the chicken breast halfway through cooking. 6. Heat the milk mixture over medium-high heat; bring to a rapid boil, stirring continuously. 7. Reduce to simmer and add the salt, and pepper; continue to cook 12 minutes more. 8. Spoon the sauce over the warm snapper fillets and serve immediately. Bon appétit!

Per Serving: Calories 429; Fat 24.09g; Sodium 236mg; Carbs 6.78g; Fibre 1.8g; Sugar 4.01g; Protein 46.49g

Spicy Prawns Kebabs

Prep time: 25 minutes | Cook time: 5 minutes | Serves: 4

675g jumbo prawns, cleaned, shelled and deveined
455g cherry tomatoes
2 tablespoons butter, melted
1 tablespoons Sriracha sauce
Sea salt and ground black pepper, to taste

½ teaspoon dried oregano
½ teaspoon dried basil
1 teaspoon dried parsley flakes
½ teaspoon marjoram
½ teaspoon mustard seeds

1. Toss all ingredients in a mixing bowl until the prawns and tomatoes are covered on all sides. 2. Soak the wooden skewers in water for 15 minutes. 3. Thread the jumbo prawns and cherry tomatoes onto skewers. 4. Insert the crisper plates in the baskets. Divide the skewers between the baskets in zone 1 and zone 2. 5. Select AIR FRY mode, adjust the cooking temperature to 205°C and set the cooking time to 5 minutes. 6. Press the MATCH COOK button and copy the zone 1 settings to zone 2. 7. Press the START/PAUSE button to begin cooking. 8. Serve warm.

Per Serving: Calories 268; Fat 17.81g; Sodium 1329mg; Carbs 29.34g; Fibre 7g; Sugar 15.32g; Protein 3.33g

Crumbed Fish Fillets

Prep time: 25 minutes | Cook time: 20 minutes | Serves: 4

2 eggs, beaten
½ teaspoon tarragon
4 fish fillets, halved
2 tablespoons dry white wine

35g parmesan cheese, grated
1 teaspoon seasoned salt
⅓ teaspoon mixed peppercorns
½ teaspoon fennel seed

1. Add the parmesan cheese, salt, peppercorns, fennel seeds, and tarragon to your food processor; blitz for about 20 seconds. 2. Drizzle fish fillets with dry white wine. Dump the egg into a shallow dish. 3. Coat the fish fillets with the beaten egg on all sides; then, coat them with the seasoned cracker mix. 4. Insert the crisper plates in the baskets. Divide the batter between the baskets in zone 1 and zone 2. 5. Select AIR FRY mode, adjust the cooking temperature to 175°C and set the cooking time to 17 minutes. 6. Press the MATCH COOK button and copy the zone 1 settings to zone 2. 7. Press the START/PAUSE button to begin cooking. 8. Serve warm.

Per Serving: Calories 306; Fat 17.82g; Sodium 855mg; Carbs 6.53g; Fibre 0.2g; Sugar 0.36g; Protein 28.02g

Smoked White Fish

Prep time: 20 minutes | Cook time: 15 minutes | Serves: 4

½ tablespoon yogurt
45g spring garlic, finely chopped
Fresh chopped chives, for garnish
3 eggs, beaten
½ teaspoon dried dill weed
1 teaspoon dried rosemary
60g spring onions, chopped

45g smoked white fish, chopped
1 ½ tablespoons crème fraîche
1 teaspoon salt
1 teaspoon dried marjoram
⅓ teaspoon ground black pepper, or more to taste
Cooking spray

1. Spritz four oven-safe ramekins with cooking spray. 2. Divide smoked whitefish, spring garlic, and spring onions among greased ramekins. 3. Crack an egg into each ramekin; add the crème, yogurt and all seasonings. 4. Insert the crisper plate in the basket in zone 1, and transfer the ramekins to it. 5. Select AIR FRY mode, adjust the cooking temperature to 180°C and set the cooking time to 13 minutes. 6. Press the START/PAUSE button to begin cooking. 7. Garnish the dish with fresh chives and enjoy.
Per Serving: Calories 156; Fat 8.68g; Sodium 671mg; Carbs 8.4g; Fibre 0.7g; Sugar 3.67g; Protein 11.19g

Parmesan Baked Tilapia

Prep time: 20 minutes | Cook time: 10 minutes | Serves: 6

100g parmesan cheese, grated
1 teaspoon paprika
1 teaspoon dried dill weed
900g tilapia fillets

80g mayonnaise
½ tablespoon lime juice
Salt and ground black pepper, to taste

1. Mix the mayonnaise, parmesan, paprika, salt, black pepper, and dill weed until everything is thoroughly combined. 2. Drizzle the tilapia fillets with the lime juice. 3. Cover each fish fillet with Parmesan mixture; roll them in parmesan mixture. 4. Insert the crisper plates in the baskets. Divide the tilapia fillets between the baskets in zone 1 and zone 2. 5. Select BAKE mode, adjust the cooking temperature to 170°C and set the cooking time to 10 minutes. 6. Press the MATCH COOK button and copy the zone 1 settings to zone 2. 7. Press the START/PAUSE button to begin cooking. 8. Serve warm.
Per Serving: Calories 262; Fat 11.48g; Sodium 482mg; Carbs 3.84g; Fibre 0.4g; Sugar 0.57g; Protein 36.13g

Fish Patties with Green Beans

Prep time: 1 hour 20 minutes | Cook time: 15 minutes | Serves: 4

455g whitefish fillets, minced
225g green beans, finely chopped
80g spring onions, chopped
1 chili pepper, deveined and minced
1 tablespoon red curry paste
1 tablespoon fish sauce

2 tablespoons apple cider vinegar
1 teaspoon water
Sea salt flakes, to taste
½ teaspoon cracked black peppercorns
2 tablespoons butter, at room temperature
½ teaspoon lemon

1. Combine all ingredients in the order listed above to the mixing dish. 2. Form the mixture into small cakes and chill for 1 hour. 3. Insert the crisper plate in the basket in zone 1, and line it with a piece of aluminum foil. 4. Place the cakes on the foil. 5. Select AIR FRY mode, adjust the cooking temperature to 200°C and set the cooking time to 15 minutes. 6. Press the START/PAUSE button to begin cooking. 7. Flip the cakes after 10 minutes of cooking time. 8. Mound a cucumber relish onto the plates; add the fish cakes and serve warm.
Per Serving: Calories 232; Fat 12.93g; Sodium 501mg; Carbs 5.64g; Fibre 2.4g; Sugar 1.59g; Protein 23.26g

Coconut Prawns

Prep time: 25 minutes | Cook time: 15 minutes | Serves: 4

⅓ teaspoon paprika
3 egg whites
35g unsweetened coconut, shredded
1 teaspoon salt
12 large prawns, peeled and de-veined

50g flaxseed meal
Lime slices, for garnish
A pinch of ground allspice
Grated zest of ½ small-sized lime

1. Dump the flaxseed meal into the first bowl. 2. Beat the eggs whites in another bowl. 3. In the third bowl, combine the coconut, lime zest, allspice, salt and paprika. 4. Dredge your prawns in the flaxseed mixture; then, coat them with egg whites on all sides; lastly, press them into the coconut mixture. Make sure to coat them well. 5. Spritz each prawns on all sides with cooking oil. 6. Insert the crisper plates in the baskets. Divide the prawns between the baskets in zone 1 and zone 2. 7. Select AIR FRY mode, adjust the cooking temperature to 200°C and set the cooking time to 11 minutes. 8. Press the MATCH COOK button and copy the zone 1 settings to zone 2. 9. Press the START/PAUSE button to begin cooking. 10. Adjust the cooking temperature to 170°C after 8 minutes of cooking time. 11. Serve the dish with lime slices.
Per Serving: Calories 148; Fat 9.18g; Sodium 769mg; Carbs 8.67g; Fibre 6.1g; Sugar 1.32g; Protein 9.64g

Fish Strips with Dijon Sauce

Prep time: 15 minutes | Cook time: 15 minutes | Serves: 4

For the Fish
455g white fish, cut into strips
1 ½ tablespoons olive oil
½ teaspoon garlic salt
1 teaspoon red pepper flakes, crushed
For the Dijon Sauce
1½ tablespoons Dijon mustard
120g mayonnaise

½ teaspoon dried dill weed
60g coconut flour
50g Parmesan cheese, grated
2 medium-sized eggs, well whisked

½ teaspoon lemon juice, freshly squeezed

1. Rub the fish strips with olive oil, salt, red pepper and dill weed. Then, prepare three shallow bowls. 2. Put the coconut flour into the first bowl. In another shallow bowl, place the eggs; in the third one, the parmesan cheese. 3. Cover the fish strips with the coconut flour, and then with the eggs; finally, roll each fish piece over the parmesan cheese. 4. Insert the crisper plate in the basket in zone 1, and transfer the fish strips to it. 5. Select AIR FRY mode, adjust the cooking temperature to 180°C and set the cooking time to 10 minutes. 6. Press the START/PAUSE button to begin cooking. 7. Flip the fish strips halfway through cooking. 8. Make the sauce by mixing together all the sauce ingredients. Serve as a dipping sauce and enjoy!
Per Serving: Calories 340; Fat 23.08g; Sodium 630mg; Carbs 4.54g; Fibre 0.9g; Sugar 1.23g; Protein 27.6g

Filipino Bangus

Prep time: 10 minutes | Cook time: 10 minutes | Serves: 4

A belly of 2 milkfish, deboned and sliced into 4 portions pieces
¾ teaspoon salt
¼ teaspoon ground black pepper
¼ teaspoon cumin powder
2 tablespoons calamansi juice
2 lemongrass, trimmed and cut crosswise into small

120ml rice wine
2 tablespoons fish sauce (Patis)
1 teaspoon garlic powder
120ml chicken stock
2 tablespoons olive oil

1. Pat the fish dry using kitchen towels. Put the fish into a large-sized mixing dish; add the remaining ingredients and marinate for 3 hours in the refrigerator. 2. Insert the crisper plate in the basket in zone 1, and transfer the fish pieces to it. 3. Select AIR FRY mode, adjust the cooking temperature to 170°C and set the cooking time to 9 minutes. 4. Press the START/PAUSE button to begin cooking. 5. Flip the food after 5 minutes of cooking time. 6. Serve the dish over mashed cauliflower and enjoy!
Per Serving: Calories 257; Fat 17.26g; Sodium 1305mg; Carbs 9.93g; Fibre 3.2g; Sugar 1.48g; Protein 19.49g

Celery Fish Burgers

Prep time: 60 minutes | Cook time: 10 minutes | Serves: 4

2 cans canned tuna fish
2 celery stalks, trimmed and finely chopped
1 egg, whisked
50g Parmesan cheese, grated

1 teaspoon whole-grain mustard
½ teaspoon sea salt
¼ teaspoon freshly cracked black peppercorns
1 teaspoon paprika

1. Mix all of the above ingredients in the order listed above; mix to combine well and shape into four cakes; chill the cakes for 50 minutes. 2. Insert the crisper plate in the basket in zone 1, and transfer the cakes to it. 3. Select ROAST mode, adjust the cooking temperature to 180°C and set the cooking time to 8 minutes. 4. Press the START/PAUSE button to begin cooking. 5. Flip the cakes halfway through cooking. 6. You can serve the dish over mashed potatoes.
Per Serving: Calories 161; Fat 6.79g; Sodium 753mg; Carbs 3.06g; Fibre 0.4g; Sugar 0.36g; Protein 22.03g

Prawns with Chipotle Sauce

Prep time: 10 minutes | Cook time: 7 minutes | Serves: 4

12 jumbo prawns
½ teaspoon garlic salt
For the Sauce
1 teaspoon Dijon mustard
4 tablespoons mayonnaise
1 teaspoon lemon rind, grated

¼ teaspoon freshly cracked mixed peppercorns

1 teaspoon chipotle powder
½ teaspoon cumin powder

1. Season your prawns with garlic salt and cracked peppercorns. 2. Insert the crisper plate in the basket in zone 1, and transfer the prawns to it. 3. Select AIR FRY mode, adjust the cooking temperature to 200°C and set the cooking time to 7 minutes. 4. Press the START/PAUSE button to begin cooking. 5. Flip the prawns after 5 minutes of cooking time. 6. Mix all ingredients for the sauce. 7. Serve with the warm prawns.
Per Serving: Calories 246; Fat 6.04g; Sodium 401mg; Carbs 1.33g; Fibre 0.3g; Sugar 0.22g; Protein 46.66g

Easy Crab Burgers

Prep time: 2 hours 20 minutes | Cook time: 15 minutes | Serves: 3

2 eggs, beaten
1 shallot, chopped
2 garlic cloves, crushed
1 tablespoon olive oil
1 teaspoon yellow mustard
1 teaspoon fresh coriander, chopped

250g crab meat
1 teaspoon smoked paprika
½ teaspoon ground black pepper
Sea salt, to taste
75g parmesan cheese

1. In a mixing bowl, thoroughly combine the eggs, shallot, garlic, olive oil, mustard, coriander, crab meat, paprika, black pepper, and salt. Mix until well combined. 2. Shape the mixture into 6 patties. Roll the crab patties over grated parmesan cheese, coating well on all sides. Place in the refrigerator for 2 hours. 3. Spritz the crab patties with cooking oil on both sides. 4. Insert the crisper plate in the basket in zone 1, and transfer the crab patties to it. 5. Select AIR FRY mode, adjust the cooking temperature to 180°C and set the cooking time to 14 minutes. 6. Press the START/PAUSE button to begin cooking. 7. Serve on dinner rolls if desired.
Per Serving: Calories 538; Fat 20.88g; Sodium 601mg; Carbs 42.81g; Fibre 17.1g; Sugar 1.21g; Protein 49.63g

Greek Monkfish with Vegetables

Prep time: 20 minutes | Cook time: 20 minutes | Serves: 2

2 teaspoons olive oil
120g celery, sliced
2 peppers, sliced
1 teaspoon dried thyme
½ teaspoon dried marjoram
½ teaspoon dried rosemary

2 monkfish fillets
1 tablespoon soy sauce
2 tablespoons lime juice
Coarse salt and ground black pepper, to taste
1 teaspoon cayenne pepper
90g Kalamata olives, pitted and sliced

1. In a nonstick frying pan , heat the olive oil for 1 minute. Once hot, sauté the celery and peppers for about 4 minutes until tender. Sprinkle them with thyme, marjoram, and rosemary and set aside. 2. Toss the fish fillets with the soy sauce, lime juice, salt, black pepper, and cayenne pepper. 3. Insert the crisper plate in the basket in zone 1, and transfer the fish fillets to it. 4. Select BAKE mode, adjust the cooking temperature to 180°C and set the cooking time to 12 minutes. 5. Press the START/PAUSE button to begin cooking. 6. Flip the fillets halfway through cooking. 7. Serve with the sautéed vegetables on the side. Bon appétit!
Per Serving: Calories 489; Fat 16.84g; Sodium 495mg; Carbs 13.99g; Fibre 3.5g; Sugar 6.01g; Protein 68.45g

Fish with Tomato

Prep time: 25 minutes | Cook time: 15 minutes | Serves: 4

2 tablespoons sunflower oil
455g fish, chopped
2 red chilies, chopped
1 tablespoon coriander powder
1 teaspoon red curry paste
240ml coconut milk

Salt and white pepper, to taste
½ teaspoon fenugreek seeds
1 shallot, minced
1 garlic clove, minced
1 ripe tomato, pureed

1. Air-fry the fish at 190°C for 10 minutes on both sides. 2. Transfer to a suitable baking pan that is previously greased with the sunflower oil. Add the remaining ingredients. 3. Place the pan in the basket and ROAST the food at 175°C for 12 minutes. 4. Serve warm.
Per Serving: Calories 310; Fat 20.04g; Sodium 148mg; Carbs 8.44g; Fibre 1.4g; Sugar 6.1g; Protein 24.03g

Fish Packets

Prep time: 20 minutes | Cook time: 15 minutes | Serves: 2

2 snapper fillets
1 shallot, peeled and sliced
2 garlic cloves, halved
1 pepper, sliced
1 small-sized Serrano pepper, sliced
1 tomato, sliced

1 tablespoon olive oil
¼ teaspoon freshly ground black pepper
½ teaspoon paprika
Sea salt, to taste
2 bay leaves

1. Place two parchment sheets on a working surface. Place the fish in the centre of one side of the parchment paper. 2. Top them with the shallot, garlic, peppers, and tomato. Drizzle olive oil over the fish and vegetables. Season them with black pepper, paprika, and salt. Add the bay leaves. 3. Fold over the other half of the parchment. Fold the paper around the edges tightly and create a half moon shape, sealing the fish inside. 4. Insert the crisper plate in the basket in zone 1, and transfer the food to it. 5. Select AIR FRY mode, adjust the cooking temperature to 200°C and set the cooking time to 15 minutes. 6. Press the START/PAUSE button to begin cooking. 7. Serve warm.
Per Serving: Calories 301; Fat 9.9g; Sodium 221mg; Carbs 5.42g; Fibre 1.2g; Sugar 1.95g; Protein 45.76g

Zingy Salmon Steaks

Prep time: 20 minutes | Cook time: 12 minutes | Serves: 2

2 salmon steaks
Coarse sea salt, to taste
¼ teaspoon freshly ground black pepper, or more to taste
1 tablespoon sesame oil
Zest of 1 lemon

1 tablespoon fresh lemon juice
1 teaspoon garlic, minced
½ teaspoon smoked cayenne pepper
½ teaspoon dried dill

1. Pat dry the salmon steaks with a kitchen towel. 2. In a ceramic dish, combine the remaining ingredients until everything is well whisked. 3. Add the salmon steaks to the ceramic dish and let them sit in the refrigerator for 1 hour. 4. Insert the crisper plate in the basket in zone 1, and transfer the salmon steaks to it. 5. Select AIR FRY mode, adjust the cooking temperature to 190°C and set the cooking time to 12 minutes. 6. Press the START/PAUSE button to begin cooking. 7. Flip the salmon steaks halfway through cooking. 8. Cook the marinade in a small sauté pan over a moderate flame until the sauce has thickened. 9. Pour the sauce over the steaks and serve.
Per Serving: Calories 547; Fat 21.97g; Sodium 276mg; Carbs 3.2g; Fibre 0.4g; Sugar 0.86g; Protein 80.1g

Prawns Scampi

Prep time: 20 minutes | Cook time: 10 minutes | Serves: 4

2 egg whites
60g coconut flour
100g Parmigiano-Reggiano, grated
½ teaspoon celery seeds
½ teaspoon porcini powder
½ teaspoon onion powder

1 teaspoon garlic powder
½ teaspoon dried rosemary
½ teaspoon sea salt
½ teaspoon ground black pepper
675g prawns, deveined

1. Whisk the egg with coconut flour and Parmigiano-Reggiano. Add in seasonings and mix to combine well. 2. Dip your prawns in the batter. Roll until they are covered on all sides. 3. Insert the crisper plates in the baskets. Divide the prawns between the baskets in zone 1 and zone 2. 4. Select ROAST mode, adjust the cooking temperature to 200°C and set the cooking time to 7 minutes. 5. Press the MATCH COOK button and copy the zone 1 settings to zone 2. 6. Press the START/PAUSE button to begin cooking. 7. Serve the dish with lemon wedges if desired.
Per Serving: Calories 296; Fat 9.45g; Sodium 2282mg; Carbs 6.17g; Fibre 0.6g; Sugar 1.25g; Protein 44.17g

Halibut Cakes with Mayo Sauce

Prep time: 20 minutes | Cook time: 10 minutes | Serves: 4

Halibut Cakes
455g halibut
2 tablespoons olive oil
½ teaspoon cayenne pepper
¼ teaspoon black pepper
Salt, to taste
Mayo Sauce
1 teaspoon horseradish, grated

2 tablespoons coriander, chopped
1 shallot, chopped
2 garlic cloves, minced
100g Romano cheese, grated
1 egg, whisked
1 tablespoon Worcestershire sauce

120g mayonnaise

1. Mix all ingredients for the halibut cakes in a bowl; knead with your hands until everything is well incorporated. 2. Shape the mixture into equally sized patties. 3. Insert the crisper plates in the baskets. Divide the cakes between the baskets in zone 1 and zone 2. 4. Select AIR FRY mode, adjust the cooking temperature to 190°C and set the cooking time to 10 minutes. 5. Press the MATCH COOK button and copy the zone 1 settings to zone 2. 6. Press the START/PAUSE button to begin cooking. 7. Flip the cakes halfway through cooking. 8. Mix the horseradish and mayonnaise. 9. Serve the halibut cakes with the horseradish mayo.
Per Serving: Calories 532; Fat 44.45g; Sodium 633mg; Carbs 3.54g; Fibre 0.6g; Sugar 1.35g; Protein 28.63g

Hake Fillets with Garlic Sauce

Prep time: 20 minutes | Cook time: 15 minutes | Serves: 3

3 hake fillets
6 tablespoons mayonnaise
1 teaspoon Dijon mustard
1 tablespoon fresh lime juice
Garlic Sauce
60g Greek-style yogurt
2 tablespoons olive oil

100g parmesan cheese, grated
Salt, to taste
¼ teaspoon ground black pepper, or more to taste

2 cloves garlic, minced
½ teaspoon tarragon leaves, minced

1. Pat the hake fillets dry. 2. In a shallow bowl, whisk together the mayonnaise, mustard, and lime juice. 3. In another shallow bowl, thoroughly combine the parmesan cheese with salt, and black pepper. 4. Dip the fish fillets in the mayo mixture; then, press them over the parmesan mixture. 5. Insert the crisper plate in the basket in zone 1, and transfer the fillets to it. 6. Select ROAST mode, adjust the cooking temperature to 200°C and set the cooking time to 10 minutes. 7. Press the START/PAUSE button to begin cooking. 8. Flip the fillets halfway through cooking. 9. Whisk all the sauce ingredients. 10. Serve the warm fish fillets with the sauce on the side. Bon appétit!
Per Serving: Calories 582; Fat 43.87g; Sodium 1330mg; Carbs 15.75g; Fibre 5.7g; Sugar 2.22g; Protein 31.83g

Cod Fillets with Avocado Mayo Sauce

Prep time: 20 minutes | Cook time: 15 minutes | Serves: 2

2 cod fish fillets
1 egg
Sea salt, to taste
2 teaspoons olive oil
½ avocado, peeled, pitted, and mashed
1 tablespoon mayonnaise
3 tablespoons sour cream

½ teaspoon yellow mustard
1 teaspoon lemon juice
1 garlic clove, minced
¼ teaspoon black pepper
¼ teaspoon salt
¼ teaspoon hot pepper sauce

1. Pat the fish fillets dry. 2. Beat the egg in a shallow bowl. Add in the salt and olive oil. 3. Dip the fish into the egg mixture, making sure to coat thoroughly. 4. Insert the crisper plate in the basket in zone 1, and transfer the fillets to it. 5. Select AIR FRY mode, adjust the cooking temperature to 180°C and set the cooking time to 12 minutes. 6. Press the START/PAUSE button to begin cooking. 7. Make the avocado sauce by mixing the remaining ingredients in a bowl. Place in your refrigerator until ready to serve. 8. Serve the fish fillets with chilled avocado sauce on the side. Bon appétit!

Per Serving: Calories 318; Fat 21.52g; Sodium 877mg; Carbs 7.28g; Fibre 3.6g; Sugar 0.86g; Protein 24.47g

Pollock with Kalamata Olives

Prep time: 20 minutes | Cook time: 15 minutes | Serves: 3

2 tablespoons olive oil
1 red onion, sliced
2 cloves garlic, chopped
1 Florina pepper, deveined and minced
3 Pollock fillets, skinless
2 ripe tomatoes, diced

12 Kalamata olives, pitted and chopped
2 tablespoons capers
1 teaspoon oregano
1 teaspoon rosemary
Sea salt, to taste
120ml white wine

1. Heat the oil in a baking pan. Once hot, sauté the onion, garlic, and pepper for 2 to 3 minutes or until fragrant. 2. Add the fish fillets to the baking pan. 3. Top them with the tomatoes, olives, and capers. 4. Sprinkle them with the oregano, rosemary, and salt. Pour in white wine and transfer to the basket. 5. Select BAKE mode, adjust the cooking temperature to 200°C and set the cooking time to 10 minutes. 6. Press the START/PAUSE button to begin cooking. 7. Taste for seasoning and serve on individual plates, garnished with some extra Mediterranean herbs if desired. Enjoy!

Per Serving: Calories 168; Fat 11.25g; Sodium 619mg; Carbs 6.95g; Fibre 2g; Sugar 3.59g; Protein 11.05g

Flounder Cutlets

Prep time: 15 minutes | Cook time: 15 minutes | Serves: 2

1 egg
100g Pecorino Romano cheese, grated
Sea salt and white pepper, to taste

½ teaspoon cayenne pepper
1 teaspoon dried parsley flakes
2 flounder fillets

1. Whisk the egg in a bowl until frothy. 2. In another bowl, mix Pecorino Romano cheese, and spices. 3. Dip the fillets in the egg mixture and turn to coat evenly; then, dredge in the cracker crumb mixture, turning a couple of times to coat evenly. 4. Insert the crisper plate in the basket in zone 1, and transfer the fillets to it. 5. Select AIR FRY mode, adjust the cooking temperature to 200°C and set the cooking time to 10 minutes. 6. Press the START/PAUSE button to begin cooking. 7. Flip the fillets halfway through cooking. 8. Serve warm.

Per Serving: Calories 532; Fat 34.17g; Sodium 1372mg; Carbs 17.54g; Fibre 5.7g; Sugar 2.24g; Protein 38.77g

Swordfish Steaks & Peppers

Prep time: 30 minutes | Cook time: 20 minutes | Serves: 3

3 peppers
3 swordfish steaks
1 tablespoon butter, melted
2 garlic cloves, minced

Sea salt and freshly ground black pepper, to taste
½ teaspoon cayenne pepper
½ teaspoon ginger powder

1. Insert the crisper plates in the baskets. 2. Place the peppers in zone 1 and add the swordfish steaks to zone 2. 3. Select ROAST mode, adjust the cooking temperature to 205°C and set the cooking time to 15 minutes. 4. Select zone 2, set the AIR FRY mode, and adjust the cooking temperature to 205°C and cooking time to 10 minutes. 5. Press the SMART FINISH button, and then press the START/PAUSE button to begin cooking. 5. Flip the peppers every 5 minutes. 6. Melt the butter in a small saucepan. Cook the garlic until fragrant and add the salt, pepper, cayenne pepper, and ginger powder. Cook them until everything is thoroughly heated. 7. Plate the peeled peppers and the roasted swordfish; spoon the sauce over them and enjoy.

Per Serving: Calories 254; Fat 13.06g; Sodium 144mg; Carbs 5.64g; Fibre 1g; Sugar 2.36g; Protein 27.93g

Tuna with Herbs

Prep time: 20 minutes | Cook time: 20 minutes | Serves: 4

1 tablespoon butter, melted
1 medium-sized leek, thinly sliced
1 tablespoon chicken stock
1 tablespoon dry white wine
455g tuna
½ teaspoon red pepper flakes, crushed

Sea salt and ground black pepper, to taste
½ teaspoon dried rosemary
½ teaspoon dried basil
½ teaspoon dried thyme
2 small ripe tomatoes, pureed
100g Parmesan cheese, grated

1. Melt ½ tablespoon of butter in a sauté pan over medium-high heat. Cook the leek and garlic until tender and aromatic. Add the stock and wine to deglaze the pan. 2. Grease the basket with the remaining ½ tablespoon of melted butter. 3. Place the fish in the basket. Add the seasonings. Top them with the sautéed leek mixture. Add the tomato puree. 4. Select AIR FRY mode, adjust the cooking temperature to 190°C and set the cooking time to 17 minutes. 5. Press the START/PAUSE button to begin cooking. 6. Top the dish with grated Parmesan cheese after 10 minutes. 7. Serve warm.

Per Serving: Calories 533; Fat 17.6g; Sodium 941mg; Carbs 12.43g; Fibre 1.3g; Sugar 2.96g; Protein 78.99g

Chapter 6 Snacks and Starters

Cauliflower Rice

Prep time: 5 minutes | Cook time: 20 minutes | Serves: 4

270g cauliflower, shredded
1 tablespoon coconut oil

1 teaspoon ground turmeric
½ teaspoon dried oregano

1. Grease the basket in zone 1 with coconut oil. 2. Mix cauliflower with ground turmeric and dried oregano. Put the mixture in the basket. 3. ROAST the cauliflower at 180°C for 20 minutes, tossing them halfway through cooking. 4. Serve warm.
Per Serving: Calories 52; Fat 3.65g; Sodium 24mg; Carbs 4.58g; Fibre 1.8g; Sugar 1.56g; Protein 1.62g

Cheese Portobello Patties

Prep time: 10 minutes | Cook time: 10 minutes | Serves: 4

250g. Portobello mushrooms, diced
1 egg, beaten
75g Monterey Jack cheese, shredded
1 teaspoon dried coriander

½ teaspoon white pepper
1 teaspoon avocado oil
2 tablespoons coconut flour

1. Mix mushrooms with egg, Monterey Jack cheese, coriander, white pepper, and coconut flour. 2. Make the patties from the mushroom mixture. 3. Brush the baskets with avocado oil and put the patties inside. 4. Select BAKE mode, adjust the cooking temperature to 190°C and set the cooking time to 8 minutes. 5. Press the MATCH COOK button and copy the zone 1 settings to zone 2. 6. Press the START/PAUSE button to begin cooking. 7. Flip the patties halfway through cooking.
Per Serving: Calories 344; Fat 10.7g; Sodium 170mg; Carbs 54.3g; Fibre 8.3g; Sugar 2.03g; Protein 14.33g

Cheese Cauliflower Bake

Prep time: 15 minutes | Cook time: 20 minutes | Serves: 2

90g cauliflower, chopped
2 eggs, beaten
50g Cheddar cheese, shredded

½ teaspoon chili powder
1 teaspoon coconut oil
120g heavy cream

1. Grease a suitable baking pan with coconut oil. 2. Mix cauliflower with eggs, Cheddar cheese, chili powder, and heavy cream. 3. Transfer the mixture in the prepared baking pan and flatten gently. 4. Transfer the baking pan to the basket in zone 1 and BAKE the meal at 195°C for 20 minutes.
Per Serving: Calories 402; Fat 34.4g; Sodium 362mg; Carbs 5.3g; Fibre 1.3g; Sugar 2.65g; Protein 18.64g

Coriander Tofu Cubes

Prep time: 15 minutes | Cook time: 10 minutes | Serves: 2

250g. tofu, cubed
1 teaspoon avocado oil
1 teaspoon dried coriander

½ teaspoon ground paprika
½ teaspoon ground black pepper
1 tablespoon apple cider vinegar

1. Mix avocado oil with dried coriander, ground paprika, ground black pepper, and apple cider vinegar. 2. Mix cubed tofu with avocado oil mixture and leave for 10 minutes to marinate. 3. Insert the crisper plate in the basket in zone 1, and transfer the cubed tofu to it. 4. Select AIR FRY mode, adjust the cooking temperature to 195°C and set the cooking time to 8 minutes. 5. Press the START/PAUSE button to begin cooking. 6. Flip the food halfway through cooking.
Per Serving: Calories 412; Fat 30.96g; Sodium 24mg; Carbs 16.33g; Fibre 5.9g; Sugar 4.52g; Protein 24.68g

Simple-Seasoned Brussels Sprouts

Prep time: 10 minutes | Cook time: 20 minutes | Serves: 4

455g Brussels sprouts, trimmed and halved
1 tablespoon garlic powder

1 tablespoon coconut oil
½ teaspoon ground black pepper

1. Mix Brussels sprouts with garlic powder, coconut oil, and ground black pepper. 2. Insert the crisper plate in the basket in zone 1, and transfer the food to it. 3. Select AIR FRY mode, adjust the cooking temperature to 190°C and set the cooking time to 20 minutes. 4. Press the START/PAUSE button to begin cooking. 5. Toss the food from time to time during cooking. 6. Serve warm.
Per Serving: Calories 88; Fat 3.77g; Sodium 30mg; Carbs 12.45g; Fibre 4.6g; Sugar 2.84g; Protein 4.35g

Cheddar Courgette Balls

Prep time: 15 minutes | Cook time: 6 minutes | Serves: 4

1 courgette, grated
50g Cheddar cheese, shredded
1 egg, beaten

1 teaspoon chili powder
1 teaspoon avocado oil

1. In the mixing bowl, mix courgette with cheese, egg, and chili powder. 2. Make the balls from the courgette mixture. 3. Sprinkle the courgette balls with avocado oil. 4. Insert the crisper plate in the basket in zone 1, and transfer the courgette balls to it. 5. Select AIR FRY mode, adjust the cooking temperature to 195°C and set the cooking time to 6 minutes. 6. Press the START/PAUSE button to begin cooking. 7. Serve the light brown courgette balls.
Per Serving: Calories 95; Fat 7.86g; Sodium 141mg; Carbs 0.72g; Fibre 0.3g; Sugar 0.14g; Protein 5.51g

Mustard Vegetables Mix

Prep time: 10 minutes | Cook time: 20 minutes | Serves: 4

90g cauliflower, chopped
90g broccoli, chopped
1 tablespoon mustard
1 tablespoon avocado oil

1 teaspoon chili powder
½ teaspoon dried dill
1 teaspoon apple cider vinegar

1. In the shallow bowl, mix mustard with avocado oil, chili powder, dried dill, and apple cider vinegar. 2. Insert the crisper plate in the basket in zone 1, and transfer the vegetables to it. 3. Pour the mustard mixture over the vegetables. 4. Select AIR FRY mode, adjust the cooking temperature to 195°C and set the cooking time to 20 minutes. 6. Press the START/PAUSE button to begin cooking. 7. Toss the vegetables halfway through cooking.
Per Serving: Calories 45; Fat 3.89g; Sodium 74mg; Carbs 2.34g; Fibre 1.3g; Sugar 0.64g; Protein 1.11g

Cream Spinach with Chives

Prep time: 5 minutes | Cook time: 10 minutes | Serves: 4

90g spinach, chopped
25g chives, chopped

120g heavy cream
1 teaspoon chili powder

1. Mix spinach with chives, heavy cream, and chili powder. 2. Transfer the mixture to basket in zone 1 and ROAST them at 180°C for 10 minutes. 3. Carefully mix the meal before serving.
Per Serving: Calories 61; Fat 5.79g; Sodium 43mg; Carbs 1.88g; Fibre 0.9g; Sugar 0.69g; Protein 1.27g

Tasty Mushroom Fritters

Prep time: 10 minutes | Cook time: 6 minutes | Serves: 2

100g mushrooms, grinded
1 teaspoon garlic powder
1 egg, beaten
3 teaspoons coconut flour

½ teaspoon chili powder
1 teaspoon coconut oil
1 tablespoon almond flour

1. In the mixing bowl, mix mushrooms with garlic powder, egg, coconut flour, chili powder, and almond flour. 2. Make the mushroom fritters. 3. Insert the crisper plate in the basket in zone 1, and transfer the fritters to it. 4. Spray them with oil. 5. Select AIR FRY mode, adjust the cooking temperature to 205°C and set the cooking time to 6 minutes. 6. Press the START/PAUSE button to begin cooking. 7. Flip the fritters halfway through cooking.
Per Serving: Calories 107; Fat 7.66g; Sodium 82mg; Carbs 3.96g; Fibre 1g; Sugar 1.59g; Protein 6.5g

Super-Easy Keto Risotto

Prep time: 5 minutes | Cook time: 20 minutes | Serves: 4

455g mushrooms, diced
25g Cheddar cheese, shredded
270g cauliflower, shredded
240ml beef stock

1 teaspoon dried oregano
1 teaspoon dried coriander
1 tablespoon coconut oil

1. Mix all ingredients in the air fryer basket and ROAST them at 190°C for 20 minutes. 2. Stir the risotto every 5 minutes to avoid burning. 3. Serve warm.
Per Serving: Calories 138; Fat 9.29g; Sodium 237mg; Carbs 9.21g; Fibre 3.2g; Sugar 4.43g; Protein 7.76g

Cheddar Broccoli Tots

Prep time: 15 minutes | Cook time: 8 minutes | Serves: 4

1 teaspoon mascarpone
125g Cheddar cheese, shredded
270g broccoli, chopped, boiled

¼ teaspoon onion powder
1 teaspoon avocado oil

1. In the mixing bowl, mix mascarpone with Cheddar cheese, broccoli, and onion powder. 2. Make the broccoli tots from the mixture and transfer them to the crisper plates in the baskets. 3. Sprinkle the broccoli tots with avocado oil. 4. Select BAKE mode, adjust the cooking temperature to 205°C and set the cooking time to 8 minutes. 5. Press the MATCH COOK button and copy the zone 1 settings to zone 2. 6. Press the START/PAUSE button to begin cooking.
Per Serving: Calories 79; Fat 4.42g; Sodium 401mg; Carbs 4.77g; Fibre 0.8g; Sugar 2.63g; Protein 5.72g

Broccoli Hash Brown

Prep time: 5 minutes | Cook time: 15 minutes | Serves: 4

180g broccoli, chopped
3 eggs, whisked

1 tablespoon coconut oil
1 teaspoon dried oregano

1. Mix broccoli with eggs and transfer the mixture to the basket in zone 1. 2. Add coconut oil and dried oregano. 3. ROAST the meal at 205°C for 15 minutes. Stir the meal every 5 minutes. 4. Serve warm.
Per Serving: Calories 131; Fat 10.74g; Sodium 83mg; Carbs 1.5g; Fibre 0.6g; Sugar 0.57g; Protein 7.38g

Healthy Courgette Tots

Prep time: 10 minutes | Cook time: 12 minutes | Serves: 4

3 courgettes, grated
60g coconut flour
2 eggs, beaten

1 teaspoon chili flakes
1 teaspoon salt
1 teaspoon avocado oil

1. In the bowl mix up grated carrot, salt, ground cumin, courgette, Provolone cheese, chili flakes, egg, and coconut flour. 2. Stir the mass with the help of the spoon and make the small balls. 3. Line the crisper plate in the basket with baking paper and sprinkle it with sunflower oil. 4. Put the courgette balls on the baking paper and AIR FRY them for 12 minutes at 375°F. 5. Toss the balls every 2 minutes to avoid burning.
Per Serving: Calories 84; Fat 6.13g; Sodium 684mg; Carbs 2.21g; Fibre 0.7g; Sugar 1.16g; Protein 5.01g

Aubergine Bites

Prep time: 10 minutes | Cook time: 10 minutes | Serves: 5

2 medium aubergines, trimmed, sliced
100g Parmesan, grated

1 teaspoon coconut oil, melted

1. Grease the crisper plates in the baskets with coconut oil. 2. Arrange the sliced aubergines onto the crisper plates in one layer. 3. Top them with Parmesan. 4. Select AIR FRY mode, adjust the cooking temperature to 200°C and set the cooking time to 10 minutes. 5. Press the MATCH COOK button and copy the zone 1 settings to zone 2. 6. Press the START/PAUSE button to begin cooking.
Per Serving: Calories 146; Fat 2.43g; Sodium 265mg; Carbs 21.96g; Fibre 6.6g; Sugar 8.08g; Protein 11.22g

Cream Broccoli Puree

Prep time: 10 minutes | Cook time: 20 minutes | Serves: 4

455g broccoli, chopped
1 tablespoon coconut oil

60g heavy cream
1 teaspoon salt

1. Put coconut oil in the basket. 2. Add broccoli, heavy cream, and salt. 3. ROAST the food at 185°C for 20 minutes. 4. Mash the cooked broccoli mixture until you get the soft puree.
Per Serving: Calories 80; Fat 6.73g; Sodium 622mg; Carbs 3.44g; Fibre 3.1g; Sugar 0.64g; Protein 3.75g

Seasoned Brussels Sprouts

Prep time: 10 minutes | Cook time: 15 minutes | Serves: 6

455g Brussels sprouts
1 teaspoon garlic powder
1 teaspoon ground coriander

1 tablespoon coconut oil
1 tablespoon apple cider vinegar

1. Put coconut oil in the baskets. 2. Divide Brussels sprouts, garlic powder, ground coriander, and apple cider vinegar between the baskets. 3. Select ROAST mode, adjust the cooking temperature to 200°C and set the cooking time to 13 minutes. 4. Press the MATCH COOK button and copy the zone 1 settings to zone 2. 5. Press the START/PAUSE button to begin cooking. 6. Toss the food from time to time during cooking.
Per Serving: Calories 54; Fat 2.5g; Sodium 19mg; Carbs 7.17g; Fibre 2.9g; Sugar 1.69g; Protein 2.64g

Fennel Bulb Wedges

Prep time: 5 minutes | Cook time: 15 minutes | Serves: 4

455g fennel bulb, cut into small wedges
1 teaspoon ground coriander

1 tablespoon avocado oil
½ teaspoon salt

1. Rub the fennel bulb with ground coriander, avocado oil, and salt. 2. Insert the crisper plate in the basket in zone 1, and transfer the food to it. 3. Select AIR FRY mode, adjust the cooking temperature to 200°C and set the cooking time to 15 minutes. 4. Press the START/PAUSE button to begin cooking. 5. Flip the food after 7 minutes of cooking time.

Per Serving: Calories 66; Fat 3.73g; Sodium 350mg; Carbs 8.28g; Fibre 3.5g; Sugar 4.46g; Protein 1.41g

Chopped Tempeh

Prep time: 8 minutes | Cook time: 12 minutes | Serves: 4

1 teaspoon apple cider vinegar
1 tablespoon avocado oil

¼ teaspoon ground turmeric
150g tempeh, chopped

1. Mix avocado oil with apple cider vinegar and ground turmeric. 2. Sprinkle the tempeh with turmeric mixture. 3. Insert the crisper plate in the basket in zone 1, and transfer the food to it. 4. Select AIR FRY mode, adjust the cooking temperature to 175°C and set the cooking time to 12 minutes. 5. Press the START/PAUSE button to begin cooking. 6. Toss the food halfway through cooking.

Per Serving: Calories 114; Fat 8.1g; Sodium 4mg; Carbs 4.14g; Fibre 0g; Sugar 0.01g; Protein 7.9g

Mushroom Balls

Prep time: 5 minutes | Cook time: 12 minutes | Serves: 6

¼ teaspoon ground black pepper
150g almond flour
1 teaspoon garlic powder

1 teaspoon dried rosemary
2 eggs, beaten
100g mushrooms, diced

1. In the mixing bowl, mix almond flour with garlic powder, dried rosemary, eggs, and mushrooms. 2. Make the balls from the mixture. 3. Insert the crisper plate in the basket in zone 1, and transfer the balls to it. 4. Select AIR FRY mode, adjust the cooking temperature to 180°C and set the cooking time to 12 minutes. 5. Press the START/PAUSE button to begin cooking. 6. Serve warm.

Per Serving: Calories 28; Fat 1.61g; Sodium 22mg; Carbs 1.16g; Fibre 0.3g; Sugar 0.4g; Protein 2.5g

Typical Courgette Chips

Prep time: 5 minutes | Cook time: 35 minutes | Serves: 6

3 courgettes, thinly sliced

1 teaspoon salt

1. Put the courgette slices on the crisper plates in the baskets and sprinkle them with salt. 2. Select AIR FRY mode, adjust the cooking temperature to 175°C and set the cooking time to 35 minutes. 3. Press the MATCH COOK button and copy the zone 1 settings to zone 2. 4. Press the START/PAUSE button to begin cooking. 5. Flip the slices every 5 minutes.

Per Serving: Calories 1; Fat 0.02g; Sodium 388mg; Carbs 0.17g; Fibre 0.1g; Sugar 0g; Protein 0.15g

Nori Sheets

Prep time: 10 minutes | Cook time: 5 minutes | Serves: 4

3 Nori sheets
1 teaspoon nutritional yeast

2 tablespoons water

1. Cut the Nori sheets roughly and transfer them to the crisper plates in the baskets. 2. Sprinkle the Nori sheets with water and nutritional yeast. 3. Select AIR FRY mode, adjust the cooking temperature to 190°C and set the cooking time to 5 minutes. 4. Press the MATCH COOK button and copy the zone 1 settings to zone 2. 5. Press the START/ PAUSE button to begin cooking.
Per Serving: Calories 3; Fat 0.01g; Sodium 45mg; Carbs 0.31g; Fibre 0.1g; Sugar 0.02g; Protein 0.36g

Avocado Halves

Prep time: 10 minutes | Cook time: 14 minutes | Serves: 4

1 avocado, pitted, halves
1 egg, beaten

1 tablespoon coconut shred

1. Cut the avocado halves into 4 wedges and dip in the egg. 2. Coat the avocado in coconut shred. 3. Insert the crisper plate in the basket in zone 1, and transfer the food to it. 4. Select AIR FRY mode, adjust the cooking temperature to 190°C and set the cooking time to 14 minutes. 5. Press the START/PAUSE button to begin cooking. 6. Flip the food halfway through cooking.
Per Serving: Calories 113; Fat 9.78g; Sodium 33mg; Carbs 4.68g; Fibre 3.4g; Sugar 0.59g; Protein 3.27g

Easy Mozzarella Sticks

Prep time: 10 minutes | Cook time: 4 minutes | Serves: 4

1 egg, beaten
4 tablespoons almond flour

225g Mozzarella, cut into sticks

1. Dip the mozzarella sticks in the egg and then coat them in the almond flour. 2. Insert the crisper plate in the basket in zone 1, and transfer the mozzarella sticks to it. 3. Select AIR FRY mode, adjust the cooking temperature to 205°C and set the cooking time to 4 minutes. 4. Press the START/PAUSE button to begin cooking.
Per Serving: Calories 129; Fat 3.01g; Sodium 500mg; Carbs 2.75g; Fibre 1.3g; Sugar 1.16g; Protein 22.72g

Keto Granola with Almonds

Prep time: 10 minutes | Cook time: 12 minutes | Serves: 4

1 teaspoon monk fruit
2 teaspoons coconut oil
3 pecans, chopped
1 teaspoon pumpkin pie spices

1 tablespoon coconut shred
75g almonds, chopped
1 tablespoon flax seeds

1. In the mixing bowl, mix all ingredients. 2. Make the small balls from the mixture. 3. Insert the crisper plate in the basket in zone 1, and transfer the balls to it. 4. Select AIR FRY mode, adjust the cooking temperature to 185°C and set the cooking time to 12 minutes. 5. Press the START/PAUSE button to begin cooking. 6. Flip the balls halfway through cooking. 7. Let the dish cool for a while before serving.
Per Serving: Calories 208; Fat 19.18g; Sodium 5mg; Carbs 6.69g; Fibre 3.6g; Sugar 1.63g; Protein 5.66g

Bacon Lettuce Wraps

Prep time: 10 minutes | Cook time: 4 minutes | Serves: 12

12 bacon strips
12 lettuce leaves

1 tablespoon mustard
1 tablespoon apple cider vinegar

1. AIR FRY the bacon strips in two zones at 205°C for 4 minutes, flipping them halfway through. 2. Sprinkle the bacon with mustard and apple cider vinegar and put on the lettuce. 3. Wrap the lettuce into rolls. Enjoy.
Per Serving: Calories 17; Fat 1.53g; Sodium 88mg; Carbs 0.51g; Fibre 0.2g; Sugar 0.06g; Protein 0.65g

Savory Chicken Skin

Prep time: 10 minutes | Cook time: 10 minutes | Serves: 3

150g chicken skin
1 teaspoon avocado oil

½ teaspoon ground black pepper

1. Chop the chicken skin roughly and mix it with avocado oil and ground black pepper. 2. Insert the crisper plate in the basket in zone 1, and transfer the food to it. 3. Select AIR FRY mode, adjust the cooking temperature to 190°C and set the cooking time to 10 minutes. 4. Press the START/PAUSE button to begin cooking. 5. Flip the food every 3 minutes. 6. Serve directly.
Per Serving: Calories 163; Fat 13.04g; Sodium 41mg; Carbs 0.71g; Fibre 0.1g; Sugar 0.38g; Protein 10.01g

Salmon Balls

Prep time: 15 minutes | Cook time: 15 minutes | Serves: 4

455g salmon fillet, minced
1 egg, beaten
3 tablespoons coconut, shredded

60g almond flour
1 tablespoon avocado oil
1 teaspoon dried basil

1. In the mixing bowl, mix minced salmon fillet, egg, coconut, almond flour, and dried basil. 2. Make the balls from the fish mixture. 3. Insert the crisper plate in the basket in zone 1, and transfer the balls to it; spray them with avocado oil. 4. Select AIR FRY mode, adjust the cooking temperature to 185°C and set the cooking time to 15 minutes. 5. Press the START/PAUSE button to begin cooking. 6. Serve hot.
Per Serving: Calories 240; Fat 14.15g; Sodium 529mg; Carbs 0.79g; Fibre 0.2g; Sugar 0.47g; Protein 25.79g

Popcorn Chicken Balls

Prep time: 10 minutes | Cook time: 12 minutes | Serves: 6

280g chicken mince
1 teaspoon Italian seasonings
1 egg, beaten

30g coconut flour
1 tablespoon avocado oil

1. Mix the chicken mince with Italian seasonings, egg, and coconut flour. 2. Make the small balls from the chicken mixture. Sprinkle the popcorn balls with avocado oil. 3. Insert the crisper plates in the baskets. Divide the balls between the baskets in zone 1 and zone 2. 4. Select AIR FRY mode, adjust the cooking temperature to 185°C and set the cooking time to 12 minutes. 5. Press the MATCH COOK button and copy the zone 1 settings to zone 2. 6. Press the START/PAUSE button to begin cooking. 7. Flip the food halfway through cooking.
Per Serving: Calories 208; Fat 15.35g; Sodium 115mg; Carbs 0.82g; Fibre 0.2g; Sugar 0.42g; Protein 15.65g

Pecan Balls

Prep time: 10 minutes | Cook time: 8 minutes | Serves: 6

4 pecans, grinded
3 tablespoons dried parsley
1 teaspoon onion powder

1 egg, beaten
50g Parmesan, grated

1. In the mixing bowl, mix pecans with dried basil, onion powder, egg, and Parmesan. 2. Make the balls from the mixture. 3. Insert the crisper plates in the baskets. Divide the balls between the baskets in zone 1 and zone 2. 4. Select AIR FRY mode, adjust the cooking temperature to 190°C and set the cooking time to 8 minutes. 5. Press the MATCH COOK button and copy the zone 1 settings to zone 2. 6. Press the START/PAUSE button to begin cooking. 7. Flip the food halfway through cooking. 8. Serve warm.
Per Serving: Calories 95; Fat 3.87g; Sodium 191mg; Carbs 6.72g; Fibre 0.3g; Sugar 0.48g; Protein 8.15g

Crispy Carrot Slices

Prep time: 10 minutes | Cook time: 15 minutes | Serves: 8

3 carrots, thinly sliced

1 teaspoon avocado oil

1. Coat the carrot slices with the avocado oil. 2. AIR FRY the carrot slices in two zones at 180°C for 30 minutes, flipping them every 5 minutes. 3. Serve hot.
Per Serving: Calories 5; Fat 0.57g; Sodium 1mg; Carbs 0.11g; Fibre 0g; Sugar 0.05g; Protein 0.01g

Bacon with Pickled Cucumbers

Prep time: 5 minutes | Cook time: 6 minutes | Serves: 4

4 pickled cucumbers

4 bacon slices

1. AIR FRY the bacon slices in zone 1 at 205°C for 3 minutes per side. 2. Cool the bacon and wrap pickled cucumbers in the bacon. Enjoy.
Per Serving: Calories 113; Fat 10.34g; Sodium 907mg; Carbs 1.68g; Fibre 0.8g; Sugar 0.9g; Protein 3.47g

Chicken Pies

Prep time: 15 minutes | Cook time: 10 minutes | Serves: 6

455g chicken fillet, boiled
1 tablespoon cream cheese
1 teaspoon chili powder
1 teaspoon garlic powder

6 wonton wraps
1 egg, beaten
1 tablespoon avocado oil

1. Shred the chicken fillet and mix it with cream cheese, chili powder, garlic powder, and egg. 2. Put the chicken mixture on the wonton wraps and roll them. Sprinkle the chicken pies with avocado oil. 3. Insert the crisper plates in the baskets. Divide the food between the baskets in zone 1 and zone 2. 4. Select BAKE mode, adjust the cooking temperature to 190°C and set the cooking time to 10 minutes. 5. Press the MATCH COOK button and copy the zone 1 settings to zone 2. 6. Press the START/PAUSE button to begin cooking. 7. Serve warm.
Per Serving: Calories 160; Fat 6.88g; Sodium 144mg; Carbs 5.49g; Fibre 0.3g; Sugar 0.24g; Protein 17.97g

Basil Salmon Bites

Prep time: 5 minutes | Cook time: 10 minutes | Serves: 6

455g salmon fillet, roughly chopped
1 tablespoon avocado oil

1 teaspoon dried basil
1 teaspoon ground black pepper

1. Mix chopped salmon with dried basil and ground black pepper. 2. Insert the crisper plates in the baskets. 3. Divide the patties between the baskets in zone 1 and zone 2, and sprinkle them with avocado oil. 4. Select BAKE mode, adjust the cooking temperature to 190°C and set the cooking time to 10 minutes. 5. Press the MATCH COOK button and copy the zone 1 settings to zone 2. 6. Press the START/PAUSE button to begin cooking. 7. Serve hot.
Per Serving: Calories 138; Fat 7.77g; Sodium 328mg; Carbs 0.36g; Fibre 0.2g; Sugar .01g; Protein 15.67g

Aubergine Slices

Prep time: 10 minutes | Cook time: 25 minutes | Serves: 4

1 aubergine, sliced
½ teaspoon salt

1 teaspoon nutritional yeast

1. Sprinkle the sliced aubergine with salt and nutritional yeast. 2. Insert the crisper plate in the basket in zone 1, and transfer the aubergine slices to it. 3. Select ROAST mode, adjust the cooking temperature to 180°C and set the cooking time to 25 minutes. 4. Press the START/PAUSE button to begin cooking. 5. Serve warm.
Per Serving: Calories 37; Fat 0.26g; Sodium 338mg; Carbs 8.36g; Fibre 4.2g; Sugar 4.86g; Protein 1.7g

Beef Meatballs

Prep time: 15 minutes | Cook time: 20 minutes | Serves: 6

280g beef mince
1 tablespoon dried coriander

1 egg, beaten
1 teaspoon ground black pepper

1. Mix all remaining ingredients and make the meatballs from them. 2. Insert the crisper plates in the baskets. 3. Divide the meatballs between the baskets in zone 1 and zone 2. 4. Select ROAST mode, adjust the cooking temperature to 185°C and set the cooking time to 20 minutes. 5. Press the MATCH COOK button and copy the zone 1 settings to zone 2. 6. Press the START/PAUSE button to begin cooking. 7. Serve hot.
Per Serving: Calories 185; Fat 10.01g; Sodium 63mg; Carbs 0.48g; Fibre 0.1g; Sugar 0.11g; Protein 21.67g

Mascarpone Bacon Rolls

Prep time: 10 minutes | Cook time: 8 minutes | Serves: 5

5 bacon slices
3 tablespoons mascarpone

1 teaspoon dried oregano

1. AIR FRY the bacon slices in zone 1 at 205°C for 4 minutes per side. 2. Cool the bacon slices little and sprinkle with dried oregano. 3. Spread the mascarpone over the bacon slices and roll them. 4. Enjoy.
Per Serving: Calories 106; Fat 10.22g; Sodium 122mg; Carbs 0.35g; Fibre 0.1g; Sugar 0.22g; Protein 3.28g

Chapter 7 Desserts

Lava Cake

Prep time: 20 minutes | Cook time: 12 minutes | Serves: 4

100g butter, melted
100g dark chocolate
2 eggs, lightly whisked
2 tablespoons monk fruit sweetener

2 tablespoons almond meal
1 teaspoon baking powder
½ teaspoon ground cinnamon
¼ teaspoon ground star anise

1. Spritz the sides and bottom of a baking pan with nonstick cooking spray. 2. Melt the butter and dark chocolate in a saucepan. 3. Mix the eggs and monk fruit in a bowl until frothy. 4. Pour the chocolate mixture into the egg mixture. Stir in the almond meal, baking powder, cinnamon, and star anise. Mix them until everything is well incorporated. 5. Scrape the batter into the prepared pan. 6. Transfer the pan to the basket in zone 1. 7. Select BAKE mode, adjust the cooking temperature to 190°C and set the cooking time to 11 minutes. 8. Press the START/PAUSE button to begin cooking. 9. Let the dish stand for 2 minutes. Invert on a plate while warm and serve. Bon appétit!
Per Serving: Calories 451; Fat 40.34g; Sodium 245mg; Carbs 16g; Fibre 3.4g; Sugar 7.4g; Protein 7.47g

Flax Nutmeg Cookies

Prep time: 25 minutes | Cook time: 20 minutes | Serves: 4

200g almond meal
2 tablespoons flaxseed meal
25g monk fruit
1 teaspoon baking powder
A pinch of grated nutmeg

A pinch of coarse salt
1 large egg, room temperature.
115g butter, room temperature
1 teaspoon vanilla extract

1. Mix the almond meal, flaxseed meal, monk fruit, baking powder, grated nutmeg, and salt in a bowl. 2. In a separate bowl, whisk the egg, butter, and vanilla extract. 3. Stir the egg mixture into dry mixture; mix to combine well or until it forms a nice, soft dough. 4. Roll your dough out and cut out with a cookie cutter of your choice. 5. BAKE the food in one zone at 175°C for 10 minutes and at 165°C for another 10 minutes. 6. Serve and enjoy.
Per Serving: Calories 581; Fat 54.53g; Sodium 226mg; Carbs 15.94g; Fibre 8.6g; Sugar 3.99g; Protein 13.88g

Mini Cheesecakes

Prep time: 40 minutes | Cook time: 35 minutes | Serves: 6

50g almond flour
1 ½ tablespoons unsalted butter, melted
2 tablespoons erythritol
1 (200g) package cream cheese, softened
Topping
360g sour cream
3 tablespoons powdered erythritol

50g powdered erythritol
½ teaspoon vanilla paste
1 egg, at room temperature

1 teaspoon vanilla extract

1. Thoroughly combine the almond flour, butter, and 2 tablespoons of erythritol in a mixing bowl. Press the mixture into the bottom of lightly greased custard cups. 2. Mix the cream cheese, 50 g of powdered erythritol, vanilla, and egg using an electric mixer on low speed. 3. Pour the batter into the pan, covering the crust. 4. Transfer the pan to the basket in zone 1. 5. Select BAKE mode, adjust the cooking temperature to 165°C and set the cooking time to 35 minutes. 6. Press the START/PAUSE button to begin cooking. 7. When cooked, the edges should be puffed and surface should be firm. 8. Mix the sour cream, 3 tablespoons of powdered erythritol, and vanilla for the topping; spread over the crust and allow it to cool to room temperature. 9. Transfer to your refrigerator for 6 to 8 hours. 10. Serve well chilled.
Per Serving: Calories 240; Fat 20.96g; Sodium 232mg; Carbs 7.83g; Fibre 1.1g; Sugar 1.76g; Protein 6.98g

Hazelnuts Cookies

Prep time: 20 minutes | Cook time: 10 minutes | Serves: 6

100g almond flour
60g coconut flour
1 teaspoon baking soda
1 teaspoon fine sea salt
115g butter

25g sweetener
2 teaspoons vanilla
2 eggs, at room temperature
130g hazelnuts, coarsely chopped

1. Mix the flour with the baking soda, and sea salt. 2. In the bowl of an electric mixer, beat the butter, sweetener, and vanilla until creamy. Fold in the eggs, one at a time, and mix until well combined. 3. Slowly and gradually, stir in the flour mixture. Finally, fold in the coarsely chopped hazelnuts.4. Divide the dough into small balls using a large cookie scoop; drop onto the prepared cookie sheets. 5. BAKE the food in two zones at 175°C for 10 minutes or until golden brown, rotating the pan once or twice through the cooking time. 6. Cool the dish for a couple of minutes before removing to wire racks. Enjoy!

Per Serving: Calories 328; Fat 32.3g; Sodium 774mg; Carbs 5.07g; Fibre 2.4g; Sugar 1.91g; Protein 6.7g

Peppermint Cake

Prep time: 40 minutes | Cook time: 20 minutes | Serves: 6

2 tablespoons stevia
60g coconut flour
115g butter
240g mascarpone cheese, at room temperature

100g cooking chocolate, unsweetened
1 teaspoon vanilla extract
2 drops peppermint extract

1. Beat the sugar, coconut flour, and butter in a mixing bowl. Press the mixture into the bottom of a lightly greased baking pan. 2. Transfer the pan to the basket in zone 1. 3. Select BAKE mode, adjust the cooking temperature to 175°C and set the cooking time to 18 minutes. 4. Press the START/PAUSE button to begin cooking. 5. Place it in your freezer for 20 minutes.6. Make the cheesecake topping by mixing the remaining ingredients. 7. Place this topping over the crust and allow it to cool in your freezer for a further 15 minutes. 8. Serve well chilled.

Per Serving: Calories 276; Fat 22.26g; Sodium 288mg; Carbs 13.3g; Fibre 0.7g; Sugar 10.12g; Protein 6.09g

Almond Chocolate Cookies

Prep time: 20 minutes | Cook time: 15 minutes | Serves: 10

200g almond flour
60g coconut flour
100g sweetener
125g butter, softened
1 egg, beaten

1 teaspoon vanilla essence
100g double cream
75g cooking chocolate, unsweetened
1 teaspoon cardamom seeds, finely crushed

1. In a mixing bowl, thoroughly combine the flour, sweetener, and butter. Mix until your mixture resembles breadcrumbs. 2. Gradually, add the egg and vanilla essence. Shape the dough into small balls. 3. Insert the crisper plates in the baskets. Line the crisper plates with parchment paper and divide the food between the baskets in zone 1 and zone 2. 4. Select BAKE mode, adjust the cooking temperature to 175°C and set the cooking time to 15 minutes. 5. Press the MATCH COOK button and copy the zone 1 settings to zone 2. 6. Press the START/PAUSE button to begin cooking. 7. Flip the food after 10 minutes of cooking time. 8. Transfer the freshly baked cookies to a cooling rack. 9. Melt the double cream and bakers' chocolate in the oven at 175°C, then add the cardamom seeds and stir them well. 10. Spread the filling over the cooled biscuits and sandwich together.

Per Serving: Calories 166; Fat 14.91g; Sodium 125mg; Carbs 6.75g; Fibre 0.4g; Sugar 5.09g; Protein 1.66g

Chocolate Brownies

Prep time: 30 minutes | Cook time: 22 minutes | Serves: 8

115g butter, melted
30g sweetener
2 eggs
1 teaspoon vanilla essence
2 tablespoons flaxseed meal

120g coconut flour
1 teaspoon baking powder
50g cocoa powder, unsweetened
A pinch of salt
A pinch of ground cardamom

1. Spritz the sides and bottom of a baking pan with cooking spray. 2. In a mixing dish, beat the melted butter with sweetener until fluffy. Fold in the eggs and beat again. 3. Add the vanilla, flour, baking powder, cocoa, salt, and ground cardamom. Mix them until everything is well combined. 4. Transfer them to the baking pan and then place the pan in the basket in zone 1. 5. Select BAKE mode, adjust the cooking temperature to 175°C and set the cooking time to 22 minutes. 6. Press the START/PAUSE button to begin cooking. 7. Enjoy!

Per Serving: Calories 168; Fat 15.74g; Sodium 170mg; Carbs 5.78g; Fibre 2.7g; Sugar 1.16g; Protein 4.05g

Fluffy Chocolate Cake

Prep time: 20 minutes | Cook time: 15 minutes | Serves: 6

60g butter, at room temperature
85g chocolate, unsweetened and chopped
1 tablespoon liquid stevia
180g coconut flour

A pinch of fine sea salt
2 eggs, whisked
½ teaspoon vanilla extract

1. Melt the butter, chocolate, and stevia in a saucepan over medium heat. 2. Add the other ingredients to the cooled chocolate mixture; stir to combine well. 3. Scrape the batter into a lightly greased baking pan. 4. Transfer the pan to the basket in zone 1. 5. Select BAKE mode, adjust the cooking temperature to 165°C and set the cooking time to 15 minutes. 6. Press the START/PAUSE button to begin cooking. 7. When done, the centre should be springy and a toothpick comes out dry. Enjoy!

Per Serving: Calories 133; Fat 4.35g; Sodium 146mg; Carbs 18.95g; Fibre 1.3g; Sugar 14.24g; Protein 4.03g

Coconut Orange Cake

Prep time: 30 minutes | Cook time: 15 minutes | Serves: 6

80g coconut flour
80ml coconut milk
2 tablespoons orange jam, unsweetened
115g butter
20g granulated sweetener

2 eggs
125g almond flour
½ teaspoon baking powder
⅓ teaspoon grated nutmeg
¼ teaspoon salt

1. Spritz the inside of a cake pan with the cooking spray. 2. Beat the butter with granulated sweetener until fluffy. Fold in the eggs; continue mixing until smooth. 3. Throw in the coconut flour, salt, and nutmeg; then, slowly and carefully pour in the coconut milk. 4. Add almond flour, baking powder and orange jam; mix thoroughly to create the cake batter. 5. Press the batter into the cake pan. 6. Transfer the pan to the basket in zone 1. 7. Select BAKE mode, adjust the cooking temperature to 180°C and set the cooking time to 17 minutes. 8. Press the START/PAUSE button to begin cooking. 9. Frost the cake and serve chilled. Enjoy!

Per Serving: Calories 316; Fat 21.87g; Sodium 286mg; Carbs 28.09g; Fibre 0.7g; Sugar 26.85g; Protein 3.76g

Old-Fashioned Walnut Cookies

Prep time: 40 minutes | Cook time: 15 minutes | Serves: 8

60g walnuts, ground
60g coconut flour
100g almond flour
20g sweetener

115g butter, room temperature
2 tablespoons rum
½ teaspoon pure vanilla extract
½ teaspoon pure almond extract

1. In a mixing dish, beat the butter with sweetener, vanilla, and almond extract until light and fluffy. 2. Throw in the flour and ground walnuts; add in rum. 3. Continue mixing until it forms a soft dough. 4. Cover the dish and place in the refrigerator for 20 minutes. 5. Roll the dough into small cookies and place them on a suitable cake pan; gently press each cookie. 6. Transfer the pan to the basket in zone 1. 7. Select BAKE mode, adjust the cooking temperature to 165°C and set the cooking time to 15 minutes. 8. Press the START/PAUSE button to begin cooking. 9. Serve warm.
Per Serving: Calories 147; Fat 14.86g; Sodium 107mg; Carbs 1.33g; Fibre 0.5g; Sugar 0.57g; Protein 1.04g

Coconut Chocolate Pudding

Prep time: 20 minutes | Cook time: 15 minutes | Serves: 10

115g butter
175g cooking chocolate, unsweetened
1 teaspoon liquid stevia

2 tablespoons full fat coconut milk
2 eggs, beaten
35g coconut, shredded

1. In a saucepan, melt the butter, chocolate, and stevia. Allow it to cool to room temperature. 2. Add the remaining ingredients to the chocolate mixture; stir to combine well. 3. Scrape the batter into a lightly greased baking pan. 4. Transfer the pan to the basket in zone 1. 5. Select BAKE mode, adjust the cooking temperature to 165°C and set the cooking time to 15 minutes. 6. Press the START/PAUSE button to begin cooking. 7. When done, a toothpick should come out dry and clean
Per Serving: Calories 116; Fat 11.84g; Sodium 102mg; Carbs 0.68g; Fibre 0.2g; Sugar 0.44g; Protein 2.02g

Blueberry Cupcakes

Prep time: 20 minutes | Cook time: 15 minutes | Serves: 6

3 teaspoons cocoa powder, unsweetened
95g blueberries
125g almond flour
120ml milk
115g butter, room temperature
3 eggs
150g granulated erythritol

1 teaspoon pure rum extract
½ teaspoon baking soda
1 teaspoon baking powder
¼ teaspoon grated nutmeg
½ teaspoon ground cinnamon
⅛ teaspoon salt

1. In the first bowl, thoroughly combine the erythritol, almond flour, baking soda, and baking powder, salt, nutmeg, cinnamon and cocoa powder. 2. In the second bowl, cream the butter, egg, rum extract, and milk; whisk them to combine well. 3. Add the wet mixture to the dry mixture. Fold in blueberries. 4. Press the prepared batter mixture into a lightly greased muffin tin. 5. Insert the crisper plates in the baskets. Divide the muffin tins between the baskets in zone 1 and zone 2. 6. Select BAKE mode, adjust the cooking temperature to 175°C and set the cooking time to 15 minutes. 7. Press the MATCH COOK button and copy the zone 1 settings to zone 2. 8. Press the START/PAUSE button to begin cooking. 9. Use a toothpick to check. 10. Serve warm.
Per Serving: Calories 335; Fat 21.12g; Sodium 339mg; Carbs 32.47g; Fibre 0.8g; Sugar 30.8g; Protein 5.65g

Espresso Brownies

Prep time: 40 minutes | Cook time: 35 minutes | Serves: 8

125g unsweetened chocolate, chopped into chunks
2 tablespoons instant espresso powder
1 tablespoon cocoa powder, unsweetened
125g almond butter
50g almond meal
20g sweetener
1 teaspoon pure coffee extract
For the Chocolate Mascarpone Frosting
100g mascarpone cheese, at room temperature
25g unsweetened chocolate chips
50g powdered sweetener

½ teaspoon lime peel zest
30g coconut flour
2 eggs plus 1 egg yolk
½ teaspoon baking soda
½ teaspoon baking powder
½ teaspoon ground cinnamon
⅓ teaspoon ancho chili powder

55g unsalted butter, at room temperature
1 teaspoon vanilla paste
A pinch of fine sea salt

1. Microwave the chocolate and almond butter until completely melted; allow the mixture to cool at room temperature. 2. Whisk the eggs, sweetener, cinnamon, espresso powder, coffee extract, ancho chili powder, and lime zest. 3. Add the vanilla mixture to the chocolate/butter mixture. Stir in the almond meal and coconut flour along with baking soda, baking powder and cocoa powder. 4. Press the batter into a lightly buttered cake pan. 5. Transfer the pan to the basket in zone 1. 6. Select BAKE mode, adjust the cooking temperature to 175°C and set the cooking time to 35 minutes. 7. Press the START/PAUSE button to begin cooking. 8. In the meantime, beat the butter and mascarpone cheese until creamy. Add in the melted chocolate chips and vanilla paste. 9. Gradually stir in the powdered sweetener and salt; beat until everything's well combined. 10. Lastly, frost the brownies and serve.
Per Serving: Calories 439; Fat 27.51g; Sodium 424mg; Carbs 41.99g; Fibre 2.6g; Sugar 34.17g; Protein 8.07g

Cranberries Fruitcake

Prep time: 30 minutes | Cook time: 20 minutes | Serves: 8

100g almond flour
⅓ teaspoon baking soda
⅓ teaspoon baking powder
150g erythritol
½ teaspoon ground cloves
⅓ teaspoon ground cinnamon
For Ricotta Frosting:
55g butter
120g firm Ricotta cheese
200g powdered erythritol

½ teaspoon cardamom
115g butter
½ teaspoon vanilla paste
2 eggs plus 1 egg yolk, beaten
65g cranberries, fresh or thawed
1 tablespoon browned butter

¼ teaspoon salt
Zest of ½ lemon

1. In a mixing bowl, combine the flour with baking soda, baking powder, erythritol, ground cloves, cinnamon, and cardamom. 2. In a separate bowl, whisk 115 g butter with vanilla paste; mix in the eggs until light and fluffy. 3. Add the flour mixture to the butter/egg mixture. Fold in the cranberries and browned butter. 4. Scrape the mixture into the greased cake pan. 5. Transfer the pan to the basket in zone 1. 6. Select BAKE mode, adjust the cooking temperature to 180°C and set the cooking time to 20 minutes. 7. Press the START/PAUSE button to begin cooking. 8. In a food processor, whip 55 g of the butter and Ricotta cheese until there are no lumps. 9. Slowly add the powdered erythritol and salt until your mixture has reached a thick consistency. Stir in the lemon zest; mix to combine and chill completely before using. 10. Frost the cake and enjoy!
Per Serving: Calories 195; Fat 18.34g; Sodium 296mg; Carbs 9.43g; Fibre 3.4g; Sugar 2.4g; Protein 4.26g

Berries with Pecan Streusel

Prep time: 20 minutes | Cook time: 15 minutes | Serves: 3

3 tablespoons pecans, chopped
3 tablespoons almonds, slivered
2 tablespoons walnuts, chopped
3 tablespoons granulated sweetener

½ teaspoon ground cinnamon
1 egg
2 tablespoons cold salted butter, cut into pieces
75g mixed berries

1. Mix the nuts, sweetener, cinnamon, egg, and butter until well-combined. 2. Place mixed berries on the bottom of a lightly greased baking pan. 3. Top them with the prepared topping. 4. Transfer the pan to the basket in zone 1. 5. Select BAKE mode, adjust the cooking temperature to 170°C and set the cooking time to 17 minutes. 6. Press the START/PAUSE button to begin cooking. 7. Serve the dish at room temperature.
Per Serving: Calories 309; Fat 19.25g; Sodium 175mg; Carbs 30.4g; Fibre 2g; Sugar 21.65g; Protein 6.2g

Chocolate Cake with Chocolate Frosting

Prep time: 35 minutes | Cook time: 30 minutes | Serves: 6

2 eggs, beaten
180g sour cream
100g almond flour
20g sweetener
80ml coconut oil, softened
Chocolate Frosting
115g butter, softened
25g cocoa powder

25g cocoa powder
2 tablespoons chocolate chips, unsweetened
1 ½ teaspoons baking powder
1 teaspoon vanilla extract
½ teaspoon pure rum extract

30g powdered sweetener
2 tablespoons milk

1. Mix all ingredients for the chocolate cake with a hand mixer on low speed. 2. Scrape the batter into a suitable cake pan. 3. Transfer the pan to the basket in zone 1. 4. Select BAKE mode, adjust the cooking temperature to 165°C and set the cooking time to 30 minutes. 5. Press the START/PAUSE button to begin cooking. 6. Transfer the cake to a wire rack. 7. Whip the butter and cocoa until smooth. Stir in the powdered sweetener. 8. Slowly and gradually pour in the milk until your frosting reaches desired consistency. 9. Whip them until smooth and fluffy; then, frost the cooled cake. 10. Place the dish in your refrigerator for a couple of hours. Serve well chilled.
Per Serving: Calories 409; Fat 36.49g; Sodium 194mg; Carbs 24.17g; Fibre 6.8g; Sugar 7.51g; Protein 8.41g

Blueberry Flan

Prep time: 30 minutes | Cook time: 25 minutes | Serves: 6

75g extra-fine almond flour
170g fresh blueberries
120ml coconut cream
180ml coconut milk
3 eggs, whisked
15g sweetener

10g powdered sweetener
½ teaspoon baking soda
½ teaspoon baking powder
⅓ teaspoon ground cinnamon
½ teaspoon crystalized ginger
¼ teaspoon grated nutmeg

1. Lightly grease 2 mini pie pans using a nonstick cooking spray. Lay the blueberries on the bottom of the pie pans. 2. In a saucepan over a moderate flame, heat the cream along with coconut milk until thoroughly heated. 3. Turn off the heat; mix in the flour along with baking soda and baking powder. 4. In a medium-sized mixing bowl, whip the eggs, sweetener, and spices; whip until the mixture is creamy. 5. Add the creamy milk mixture. Carefully spread this mixture over the fruits. 6. Divide the mixture between the pie pans. 7. Transfer the pans to the basket in zone 1. 8. Select BAKE mode, adjust the cooking temperature to 160°C and set the cooking time to 25 minutes. 9. Press the START/PAUSE button to begin cooking. 10. To serve, dust the food with confectioner's sweetener.
Per Serving: Calories 290; Fat 21.88g; Sodium 171mg; Carbs 19.61g; Fibre 1.9g; Sugar 16.35g; Protein 6.43g

Fluffy Pancakes

Prep time: 35 minutes | Cook time: 5 minutes | Serves: 3

60g coconut flour
1 teaspoon baking powder
¼ teaspoon salt
2 tablespoons erythritol
½ teaspoon cinnamon
Topping
50g cream cheese, softened
2 tablespoons butter, softened

1 teaspoon red paste food color
1 egg
120ml milk
1 teaspoon vanilla

25g powdered sweetener

1. Mix the coconut flour, baking powder, salt, erythritol, cinnamon, red paste food color in a large bowl. 2. Gradually add the egg and milk, whisking continuously, until well combined. Let the mixture stand for 20 minutes. 3. Spritz two suitable baking pans with cooking spray. Pour the batter into the pans. 4. Transfer the pans to the baskets in zone 1 and zone 2. 5. Select BAKE mode, adjust the cooking temperature to 160°C and set the cooking time to 5 minutes. 6. Press the MATCH COOK button and copy the zone 1 settings to zone 2. 7. Press the START/PAUSE button to begin cooking. 8. Make the topping by mixing the ingredients until creamy and fluffy. 9. Decorate the pancakes with topping and enjoy.
Per Serving: Calories 255; Fat 20.54g; Sodium 436mg; Carbs 18.69g; Fibre 7.2g; Sugar 4.9g; Protein 9.91g

Spanish Churros

Prep time: 20 minutes | Cook time: 10 minutes | Serves: 4

180ml water
1 tablespoon sweetener
¼ teaspoon sea salt
¼ teaspoon grated nutmeg

¼ teaspoon ground cloves
6 tablespoons butter
75g almond flour
2 eggs

1. Boil the water in a pan over medium-high heat; now, add the sweetener, salt, nutmeg, and cloves; cook them until dissolved. 2. Add the butter and turn the heat to low. Gradually stir in the almond flour, whisking continuously, until the mixture forms a ball. 3. Turn off the heat; fold in the eggs one at a time, stirring them to combine well. 4. Pour the mixture into a piping bag with a large star tip. 5. Squeeze 10 cm strips of dough into a suitable baking pan. 6. Transfer the pan to the basket in zone 1. 7. Select BAKE mode, adjust the cooking temperature to 210°C and set the cooking time to 6 minutes. 8. Press the START/PAUSE button to begin cooking. 9. Serve and enjoy.
Per Serving: Calories 220; Fat 22.26g; Sodium 334mg; Carbs 0.64g; Fibre 0.1g; Sugar 0.35g; Protein 4.72g

Vanilla Cupcakes

Prep time: 30 minutes | Cook time: 15 minutes | Serves: 4

60g coconut flour
80ml coconut milk
2 eggs

1 tablespoon coconut oil, melted
1 teaspoon vanilla
A pinch of ground cardamom

1. Mix the flour, coconut milk, eggs, coconut oil, vanilla, and cardamom in a large bowl. 2. Let the mixture stand for 20 minutes. 3. Spoon the batter into two greased muffin tins. 4. Transfer the muffin tins to the baskets in zone 1 and zone 2. 5. Select BAKE mode, adjust the cooking temperature to 110°C and set the cooking time to 5 minutes. 6. Press the MATCH COOK button and copy the zone 1 settings to zone 2. 7. Press the START/PAUSE button to begin cooking. 8. Decorate the cupcakes with coconut chips and enjoy.
Per Serving: Calories 151; Fat 13.07g; Sodium 86mg; Carbs 3.27g; Fibre 0.9g; Sugar 1.94g; Protein 5.21g

Walnut Crisp

Prep time: 40 minutes | Cook time: 35 minutes | Serves: 8

130g walnuts
Topping
150g almond flour
60g coconut flour
15g sweetener
1 teaspoon crystallized ginger

15g sweetener

½ teaspoon ground cardamom
A pinch of salt
115g butter, cut into pieces

1. Place walnuts and 15 g of sweetener in a suitable baking pan lightly greased with nonstick cooking spray. 2. In a mixing dish, thoroughly combine all the topping ingredients. 3. Sprinkle the topping ingredients over the walnut layer. 4. Transfer the pan to the basket in zone 1. 5. Select BAKE mode, adjust the cooking temperature to 165°C and set the cooking time to 35 minutes. 6. Press the START/PAUSE button to begin cooking. 7. Serve warm.
Per Serving: Calories 171; Fat 18.13g; Sodium 126mg; Carbs 2.11g; Fibre 0.9g; Sugar 0.68g; Protein 1.82g

Vanilla Rum Cookies with Walnuts

Prep time: 35 minutes | Cook time: 15 minutes | Serves: 6

50g almond flour
60g coconut flour
½ teaspoon baking powder
¼ teaspoon fine sea salt
115g butter, unsalted and softened

15g sweetener
1 egg
½ teaspoon vanilla
1 teaspoon butter rum flavouring
75g walnuts, finely chopped

1. In a mixing dish, thoroughly combine the flour with baking powder and salt. 2. Beat the butter and sweetener with a hand mixer until pale and fluffy; add the whisked egg, vanilla, and butter rum flavouring; mix again to combine well. Stir in the dry ingredients. 3. Fold in the chopped walnuts and mix to combine. 4. Divide the mixture into small balls; flatten each ball with a fork and transfer them to two foil-lined baking pans. 5. Transfer the pans to the baskets in zone 1 and zone 2. 6. Select BAKE mode, adjust the cooking temperature to 180°C and set the cooking time to 14 minutes. 7. Press the MATCH COOK button and copy the zone 1 settings to zone 2. 8. Press the START/PAUSE button to begin cooking. 9. Transfer the dish to wire racks to cool completely before enjoying.
Per Serving: Calories 261; Fat 26.86g; Sodium 262mg; Carbs 3.13g; Fibre 1.2g; Sugar 1.06g; Protein 3.99g

Anise Orange Cake

Prep time: 30 minutes | Cook time: 20 minutes | Serves: 6

40g hazelnuts, roughly chopped
3 tablespoons sugar free orange marmalade
115g butter
2 eggs plus 1 egg yolk, beaten
5 tablespoons liquid monk fruit
150g unbleached almond flour

1 teaspoon baking soda
½ teaspoon baking powder
½ ground anise seed
½ teaspoon ground cinnamon
½ teaspoon ground allspice
Pan oil

1. Lightly grease a suitable cake pan using a pan oil. 2. Whip the liquid monk fruit and butter in the pan; whip until pale and smooth. Fold in the eggs, hazelnuts and marmalade; beat again until everything's well mixed. 3. Throw in the almond flour, baking soda, baking powder, allspice, anise star, and ground cinnamon. 4. Transfer the pan to the basket in zone 1. 5. Select BAKE mode, adjust the cooking temperature to 155°C and set the cooking time to 20 minutes. 6. Press the START/PAUSE button to begin cooking. 7. To finish, add the frosting. Enjoy.
Per Serving: Calories 375; Fat 35.48g; Sodium 335mg; Carbs 10.5g; Fibre 4.6g; Sugar 3.92g; Protein 8.24g

Pecan Fudge Cake

Prep time: 30 minutes | Cook time: 22 minutes | Serves: 6

115g butter, melted
15g sweetener
1 teaspoon vanilla essence
1 egg
50g almond flour
½ teaspoon baking powder

25g cocoa powder
½ teaspoon ground cinnamon
¼ teaspoon fine sea salt
25g cooking chocolate, unsweetened
30g pecans, finely chopped

1. Lightly grease six silicone molds. 2. In a mixing dish, beat the melted butter with the sweetener until fluffy. Stir in the vanilla and egg and beat again. 3. Add the almond flour, baking powder, cocoa powder, cinnamon, and salt. Mix them until everything is well combined. 4. Fold in the chocolate and pecans; mix to combine. 5. Divide them among the molds. 6. Insert the crisper plates in the baskets. Divide the molds between the baskets in zone 1 and zone 2. 7. Select BAKE mode, adjust the cooking temperature to 175°C and set the cooking time to 22 minutes. 8. Press the MATCH COOK button and copy the zone 1 settings to zone 2. 9. Press the START/PAUSE button to begin cooking. 10. Serve warm.
Per Serving: Calories 210; Fat 20.5g; Sodium 240mg; Carbs 6.4g; Fibre 1.7g; Sugar 2.79g; Protein 2.81g

Cinnamon Cookies

Prep time: 60 minutes | Cook time: 15 minutes | Serves: 10

4 tablespoons liquid monk fruit
60g hazelnuts, ground
115g butter, room temperature
200g almond flour

120g coconut flour
50g granulated sweetener
2 teaspoons ground cinnamon

1. Cream liquid monk fruit with butter until the mixture becomes fluffy. Sift in both types of flour. 2. Stir in the hazelnuts. Knead the mixture to form dough; place in the refrigerator to chill it for about 35 minutes. 3. Shape the prepared dough into the bite-sized balls; arrange them on a baking dish; flatten the balls using the back of a spoon. 4. Mix granulated sweetener with ground cinnamon. Press the cookies in the cinnamon mixture until they are completely covered. 5. Insert the crisper plates in the baskets and line them with parchment paper. 6. Divide the cookies between the baskets in zone 1 and zone 2. 7. Select BAKE mode, adjust the cooking temperature to 155°C and set the cooking time to 20 minutes. 8. Press the MATCH COOK button and copy the zone 1 settings to zone 2. 9. Press the START/PAUSE button to begin cooking. 10. Leave them to cool for about 10 minutes before serving.
Per Serving: Calories 157; Fat 13.44g; Sodium 98mg; Carbs 9.34g; Fibre 1.3g; Sugar 7.72g; Protein 1.37g

Berry Compote with Coconut Chips

Prep time: 25 minutes | Cook time: 20 minutes | Serves: 6

1 tablespoon butter
150g mixed berries
10g granulated sweetener
¼ teaspoon grated nutmeg

¼ teaspoon ground cloves
½ teaspoon ground cinnamon
1 teaspoon pure vanilla extract
50g coconut chips

1. Grease a suitable baking pan with butter. 2. Place all ingredients, except for the coconut chips, in a baking pan. 3. Mix then well. 4. Transfer the pan to the basket in zone 1. 5. Select BAKE mode, adjust the cooking temperature to 165°C and set the cooking time to 20 minutes. 6. Press the START/PAUSE button to begin cooking. 7. Serve the dish in individual bowls and garnish with coconut chips.
Per Serving: Calories 227; Fat 9.8g; Sodium 148mg; Carbs 33.88g; Fibre 1.6g; Sugar 20.86g; Protein 1.5g

Conclusion

Discover the exceptional versatility of the Ninja Foodi 2-Basket Air Fryer. With a maximum temperature of 400 degrees Fahrenheit and a maximum cooking duration of one hour, you can enjoy much more than your typical air fryer can offer. The possibilities are endless, from reheating French fry leftovers to dehydrating fruits and roasting a chicken without using your oven. The two baskets make it possible to prepare two dishes simultaneously, allowing you to whip up a complete meal with just one appliance. Say goodbye to the days of settling for 25-minute air fryers and say hello to the revolutionary 8-quart capacity of the Ninja Foodi. Get ready to experience a professional level of Cooking that will make dinner time a breeze. Try it today and enjoy the convenience and quality of the Ninja Foodi.

Appendix Recipes Index

Printed in Great Britain
by Amazon

47224686R10061